LIFE JOURNEYS: STEPPING BACK AND MOVING FORWARD

SOME THOUGHTS FROM OUR SOURCES OF FAITH AND LESSONS FOR CONTEMPORARY SOCIETY AND LIFE

by

Dr. Saundra Sterling Epstein

Dedication and Acknowledgements

For our roots, we thank and have gratitude for our parents

Hannah and Ken Sterling
Rose and Willie Rosenstein
May their memories continue to bring many blessings

For taking on the wings we have tried to give, we thank and have gratitude for our children

Yoella Leah and Jeremy, Neli, Neima and Adel
Brian, Talie, Rachie and Liz

And for sharing all of these thoughts and ideas and helping me to develop them, the teachers from who I have learned so much, the colleagues and friends with whom I have shared so much and most important, the thousands of students of all ages with whom I have had the privilege of sharing so many meaningful learning journeys….

And most of all, thank you to the love of my life for sharing all of this with me, my husband, **Ken Rosenstein.**

May we all learn that our steps back into our past will guide our moving forward into our shared future.

© Dr. Saundra Sterling Epstein, BeYachad Publications, 2017

An Introductory Word or Two

Today in our world and in our country, as we confront so many different challenges and threats to our collective and individual well-being, we constantly look for support for our soul and our well-being. While religion and what one believes should and can offer such support, the degree to which it does so is often a hot controversial topic. Not of course, that this is a new phenomenon. Religion has always been so much at the core of our beings as humans, whether we individually admit this to be the case or not. In fact, in cultural and ethnographic studies, religion is one of the core markers of any people being studied. (1)

One cannot study European History, Ancient History or any other people's story and narrative without speaking of religion. For Ancient Man, as well as for many tribal and land based cultures and people today, religion is still at the core of their individual as well as collective beings. Simply, for many, if not most people throughout history, religion has been an exclamation mark – the ***Of Course!*** of their lives. This is especially true for those who are closer to the land, as the land they work and depend upon, and the Higher Being to whom they pray for sustenance from the land are clearly connected in a visceral way that is core to daily life. Religion provides responses to questions that elude us in the more tangible aspects of our lives, and as such, provides a support that is specific and unique to its context alone.

As an expression of this sentiment, look at these words of George Copway (Kahgegagahbowh) as recorded by Ken Nerburn in his important collection of teachings in The Wisdom of the Native Americans (California: New World Library, 1999):

I was born in Nature's wide domain! The trees were all that sheltered my infant limbs, the blue heavens all that covered me. I am one of Nature's children …

And whenever I see her, emotions of pleasure roll in my breast, and swell and burst like waves on the shores of the ocean, in prayer and praise to Him (God) who has placed me in her hand. It is thought great to be born in palaces, surrounded with wealth – but to be born in Nature's wide domain is greater still! (2)

For those of us in the modern industrialized and technologically advanced world, however, God and God's presence in our lives has apparently become more and more of a question mark. Namely, we ask, "Is there a Higher Being, and do I care?" Do I need a Higher Being? Do I believe? What do I believe? Why should I believe? Because we question instead of exclaim our beliefs, does this mean that religion is no longer at the core of our being?

In the throes of addressing the results of a recent survey by the Pew Forum on Religion & Public Life, we are dealing with an American population in which 16.1% claim that they do not affiliate with any religion. Further, this number is reported to be double that of those who say they were unaffiliated as children, reflecting a movement away from what would clearly be labeled normative expressions of religion in more individual lives as we continue on our present trajectory (3).

Through my career, I have had many opportunities to address these issues as an instructor, lecturer, and head of schools and educational systems and as an avid observer, as well as a self-identified person of faith. One of the seasons which I have found often raises the issue of identity with religion to the point of hyperawareness in the United States is that of the winter weeks leading up to Christmas.

There is no surprise here, given the commercialism and obvious "front and center" of the season, in addition to the obvious profound meaning of the time.

That being said, my experience has been that something else is going on. As one measure of the impact of this observance on the non-Christian members of American society, one need only observe the proliferation of options for Jewish families and community members as alternatives for this day of obvious importance to so many. Further, I have often found on an annual basis, the issue of what winter decorations and religious symbols appear in our public spaces becomes an item on the agenda of school boards and agencies as an interesting point of angst. When I held various leadership posts in different regions throughout my career, communities and individuals would often contact me about their discomfort regarding the visual evidence of the Christmas season. In my work with these communities, I tried to convey the difference between "teaching religion" and "teaching that religion as an institution with its many forms has a value" to us as individuals, groups and a national entity.

At its foundation, religion as a system of thought and faith as well as its potential in conveyance of meaningfulness to our daily lives and actions provides us with a unique and singular synergy as it touches the very core of our beings with the comfort it provides through a belief in something bigger than us and beyond the daily regimen of our busy lives, so filled with technology, industrious undertakings, and efficient use of time. Many would agree that it still remains the ***Of Course!*** in our hectic lives, whether or not we recognize it as such.

In more recent years in the United States of America, we have witnessed attempts to remove the words "under God" from our Pledge of Allegiance, legal proceedings have been pursued to remove sculptured representations of The Ten Commandments in several American cities, and stirrings are occasionally heard regarding the same feelings of discomfort having the words "In God we trust" on our currency and the various references to God in our songs of national pride. Clearly, the operational meaning of ***separation of church and state*** is being tested, retested, and perhaps even redefined in a manner far different from what we were taught was intended by the founders of these United States of America. This is somewhat ironic as we remember that the notion of our national forefathers was to permit all Americans to worship as they like and prefer, but to be free to worship nonetheless, not to the exclusion of those who wish to exercise their prerogative to not do so.

This was a radical departure from most places and spaces in our collective history of the world (as well as what is still present in many regions around our globe today), in which one's national identity, cultural life and religion were a package deal, very often defined by the ruler of the land in which one lived. The American separation of church and state was precisely intended to teach all to value the notion of religious belief in a manner most appropriate and meaningful to them – that is, to encourage religious practices and beliefs, ALL religious practices and beliefs, without the "state" determining which "church" such practices and beliefs would have to conform to for any individual.

Conversely, way over on the opposite side of the continuum of belief and meaningful living from those who would turn their back on religion and its various instructions and frames to enable and support our lives, Fundamentalism has truly become a formidable challenge for so many of us in our contemporary world. As increasing numbers of members of our society become more liberal and less rooted in their treasured past on the left side of our cultural continuum, on its right side we have compelling instances of whole groups, communities, even nations who have literally closed their eyes and minds to any shade of these more liberal, some would say less principled, approaches to life. For some, it's even simpler than that; with adherents claiming that if you do not believe exactly as I do and do as I do, you are rendered as persona non-gratis! As a result, these forces have become stubbornly rigid in what they believe to be the most stringent definition of their respective religious communities. In short, our world is increasingly being painted in black and white distinct color blocks; while many have worked so hard for generations to achieve a moderate approach of understanding that so much of life ultimately and truly happens in the variegated gray zone.

So, how do we reconcile this dynamic? How do we balance our allegiance and valuing of the past and its rootedness as well as the lessons learned from its sources with a more measured and positive outlook for our future? How do we take chances and strive for more meaning and substance in our lives in a synchronistic manner that encompasses and protects the valuing of all shades of belief systems? This is the question, which is explored here; and the search at hand, and a challenging and sometimes exhausting search it is!

I do want to note that the voice of this book is definitely based in Jewish thinking and texts. That being said, all are welcome to engage in the thinking and dialogue that I hope will evolve as a result of reading these essays. It is more about the fact that we may believe than the specifics of what that system of belief is. In that spirit, please use the Jewish texts here as emblematic of a system of belief from which the intrinsic thoughts and questions are extrapolated and feel free to do the same within other systems of belief and thought, also represented here at points.

There will be many questions in this book and it is intended that we read this thoughtfully and slowly, pausing to consider and answer these questions. Imagine reading this manuscript in a meditative mode, letting into your soul the questions, journeys and experiences of those that have gone before us as we consider the questions of our own journeys and experiences. You might even want to keep a journal nearby in which you can write your own thoughts and truly become a participant in the intended discussion that is this collection of essays and thoughts in any way that is meaningful. This book is much more about the questions asked than the various approaches provided; in fact each chapter will end with **Questions for Continued Thought and Discussion.** Welcome on what I hope will be a shared and meaningful journey, where we accept challenges that are thrown our way and use them to strengthen our own approaches in attempting to live a meaningful and important life.

Questions unite, answers divide.
Martin Buber (and attributed to so many others as well)

© Dr. Saundra Sterling Epstein, BeYachad Publications, 2017

Table of Contents

1. **Stepping Back and Moving Forward**   14
   - The value of the lessons of our past and how we should use them as strength and instruction in moving into our future; the lesson of Abraham and his leaving the life of his past to forge a new one, under the direction of the One and Only One God.

2. **Roots and Wings**   28
   - Balancing the roots of our lives and the wings that take us into new directions is examined, using various examples from our texts and lives; contemporary problems in religious communities in which both of these gifts of roots and wings are either not valued or not able to be utilized.

3. **Free Choice or Informed Choice?**   51
   - Choosing freely is both our greatest challenge and gift; how do we choose freely and wisely, using the lessons of our past and being mindful of the balance of our roots and wings? What does the nature of choice in Judaism teach us about God and our relationship to God as well as the unique nature of the human being?

4. **Rules and Regulations**   72
   - As we continue the discussion of informed choices and the use of our past and our roots in forging a

meaningful and significant future, the place of rules and regulations in our life is discussed, both specifically from a Jewish perspective and in terms of a general approach.

5. **When My Childhood is Your History** 97
    - Lessons learned from the past are revisited as part of the cumulative experience of us all, whether or not we "lived through" the indicated events; the lesson of the sixties generation is a focus, while the factors and balances already presented are continued in this exploration. Also discussed so briefly are various chapters of history in which the lessons put forth in this collection are not observed or valued and the consequences of this dynamic.

6. **Me and We** 112
    - Balancing the importance and integrity of the individual and the value and cumulative power of the group is yet another venue in which we show that we become more powerful and effective individuals by being gracious and inclusive members of the larger group. The lessons of the sixties in the previous chapter are continued in this discussion, as are important discussions from long ago by Religious Masters of the Talmud.

7. **Values and Actions** 127
    - One compelling teaching of Judaism is that our values and actions are often one and the same; and not able nor are they supposed to be teased away from each

other. The leads to a sense of responsibility and accountability – to ourselves, to the group/s of which we are members, and to God.

8. **Passion or Compassion**   144
   - Another one of the balancing acts of our lives, how do we teach and live the compassion of our religious ideals with passion that enables, not destroys? Revisiting the dynamic and institution of Fundamentalism in the world of religion and thought and the damage it has done will be part of this discussion.

9. **A Few Important and Timeless Teachers**   161
   - We learn from so many people around us, both famous and not so much. The lessons learned by this author from Golda Meir, Elisha ben Abuyah, Kohelet and Mrs. Helen Shefferman, among others, will be shared.

10. **Soft Souls in Rough Winds**   179
    - Now, how do we live out the ideals indicated here if and when we confront the reality of the world and everyone else is living by different standards? Do we give in or gather strength from what we have learned?

11. **The Greatest Teacher of All – The Power Above**   191
    - Lessons learned from believing in God, both for those who do and those who do not share this belief. The

tracking of the development of a sense of God/Higher Being/Higher Power in our lives can be an important part of our ongoing self-awareness.

12. **Achdut: Accepting and Appreciating the Gifts We All Bring** 208
    - So with our shared similarities as well as the differences that divide and define us, how do "we all play nicely on the same playground" of life and work to create a community of communities in which we share our differences and similarities? How can we develop a different model that reflects our coming together instead of the many instances of destruction and division?

13. **How to Build Our Community: A Model from the Past and Reality of the Present** 221
    - Ideas have been expressed, questions asked and approaches suggested. Truly this book could have ended with Chapter 12, but let us examine together an important model from the Jewish Talmud about how we think about community and the many challenges building it presents to us in the practicality of our lives today and with the consideration of present concerns.

Appendix I: Endnotes and Sources to Consult for More Information 238

Appendix II: Glossary of Hebrew Terms 251

1. Stepping Back and Moving Forward

"God said to Avram, "Go for your sake, leave from your land, from your birthplace, and from the house of your father; go to the land that I will show you."
Genesis, Chapter 12, verse 1(4)

Abraham is traditionally regarded as the first Jew, certainly within the Jewish world and the history that defines it. However, within the larger context of world history and those dedicated to its study, the title "the first Jew" while an interesting retrospective is considered by many to be somewhat problematic as Judaism and the system of laws and practices that define it had certainly not yet been formulated at the time of Abraham's life, but rather many years later as it became associated with the people that observed them. To be sure, this is always a problem in terms of a developing ideology and tracing its inception accurately and with historical integrity back to its first adherent. For example, one could certainly make a similar case for Jesus, associated and credited with the beginning of Christianity.

Nonetheless, within this larger stage one could (and many have, including Tom Cahill in his book, The Gifts of the Jews, New York: Doubleday, 1998) clearly ascertain that Abraham brought the powerful and groundbreaking idea of monotheism, that is the ultimate and complete faith and belief in as well as accountability to One and Only One God, The Creator of All, and all that entails in terms of our behaviors and the initiatives that we take, to our world in a pivotal moment of our history. This is innovative in that Avram/Avraham/Abraham will break with the pattern of repetition of the ongoing "cyclical nature of reality." Cahill imagines that people had to "have laughed at Avram's madness and pointed to the

14

heavens, where the life of earth had been plotted from all eternity." Who was this guy, with the barren wife, kidding – he was going to change the trajectory of the human journey and think outside of the lines; or the predetermined circle of life in this case? (5)

This was a significant departure from the generations that preceded him with their understanding of a multiplicity of deities and their various realms of control and dominion, all with defined boundaries and territories to which adherents were responsible and by which they were controlled and from which they could not escape and take their own initiative. All were subject to the predictable journey and its defined chapters on the Great Wheel of Life and Death, that cyclical pattern from which there was no escape according to many cultures and their religious systems. For example, it is well known that in Ancient Egypt, there was a complex system of multiple deities that controlled each and every aspect of nature and realm of human activity. In fact, it should be pointed out that to truly separate from this established and normative pattern of religious life, and its known practices, was not so simple. As an example even in the monotheistic narrative of the Jewish nation and its coming to be in the chapters of Torah, we do see evidence of vestiges of idols and their worship through the Genesis narrative and beyond.

Within the context of this reality, the notion that all that we have and are comes from One Being, Force or Source that many refer to as God was wholly new, many would say creative and innovative, even radical. Simultaneously, others would find this idea of this One Supreme Being that is so much larger and greater than any of us to be discomforting and confusing. Acceptance of this novel concept forces us to address so many questions about such a Supreme Being, while relating to a God that appears to be intangible and not represented specifically by any physical entity. Further, we must confront issues of accountability if indeed all that is and we know to be emanates from One and Only One Source.

So how exactly did this one person whom we take to be Abraham accomplish this feat and leave such a legacy for us all? What happened to incite such an incredible, and perhaps counter-intuitive, action on his part? In the beginning of chapter twelve of the first book of the Torah or Jewish Bible named **Bereshit** (in Hebrew) or Genesis, we read the following words:

> *Lech Lecha MeArtzecha, u'MeMoladitecha, u'MeBet Avecha*
> Go for your own sake, from your land, and from your birthplace, and from the house of your father (Genesis 12.1)

These words are intriguing and powerful on a multitude of levels, having inspired interpretations and suggested significance by many who study such texts. Let's begin by looking at the words themselves as translated above. God tells Avram (the original name of our hero before God later changed it to Avraham or Abraham) to "go for your sake" or *lech lecha*. For your own well-being, says God to Avram, leave all of the places and people that you know and love – the land in which you have lived, the place in which you were born and the people and familiar sights of the home of your father and those whom you have loved, never to return.

In Jewish thinking and teaching this is a very directed and focused journey. Cahill suggests otherwise, when he writes as follows:

> So, *"vayelech Avram" ("Avram went")* – [are] two of the boldest words in all literature. They signal a complete departure from everything that has gone before in the long evolution of culture and sensibility. Out of Sumer, civilized repository of the predictable, comes a man who does not know where he is going but goes forth into the unknown wilderness under the prompting of his god. Out of

Mesopotamia, home of the canny, self-serving merchants who use their gods to ensure prosperity and favor, comes a wealthy caravan with no material goal. Out of ancient humanity, which from the dim beginnings of its consciousness has read its eternal verities in the starts, comes a party traveling by no known compass. Out of the human race, which knows in its bones that all its striving must end in death, comes a leader who says he has been given an impossible promise." (6)

What is so remarkable for Cahill in terms of Avram's actions is that there is "no known compass" for his journey. For Jewish history and that of all of monotheistic Children of Abraham, there was to be a different compass based on this set of instructions – this is a most important point of distinction.

One of the many medieval Jewish commentators who try to explain the complexities of the sacred text of Torah and its meanings, Rabbi Shlomo ben Isaac or **Rashi** who lived in the eleventh and twelfth centuries, also draws our attention to the order in which this statement of departure for Avram is made. He reminds us that each of the places that Avram is instructed to leave is increasingly difficult to separate from – first the land in which he lived and has grown to know so well is hard to move away from, then his birthplace to which he would be emotionally attached is even more difficult to leave, and finally his father's home is almost impossible to tear away from, knowing with certainty that he will not return to this place for the remainder of his life, as was the reality of his time. Simply, he is to leave all that he has known and with which he is familiar and confident and all that he has been up to this point in his life, so that he may follow this One Supreme God who is intangible, so to speak. Further, it will be in this One Supreme God that Avram places all trust and his very being for safekeeping as he embarks on his journey into a completely unknown future, except for the protection of his faith in God, which of course is the point.

It is clearly reasonable for us to ask ourselves how such a difficult task could possibly be for someone's sake, that is, for their own good. Can difficult and painful challenges be *for our good*? But of course, we know that this is possible, even a significant factor of reality. In fact, many of us come to understand that these very experiences may often be the most poignant and important occurrences in our lives and produce the most compelling lessons that will ultimately define our lives and the path we take as we continue our journey through this world. Our psychologists teach about this phenomenon, represented in these words by Melanie A. Greenberg, Ph.D. in an article in Psychology Today from March 4, 2013:

> Experiencing a traumatic event ... can be emotionally devastating. For some people, who do not have proper emotional support at the time of the trauma, the event can get "stuck: in their nervous systems leading to long-lasting distress ... There can be another side to stressful life experiences, however. Research shows that many people report psychological growth and positive psychological changes resulting from highly stressful events. This growth does not "undo" the negative effects, but may co-exist with them, or may be the result of therapeutic or spiritual work. (7)

Let's look closer at the events that unfold in our story and think about this situation and its ramifications, as well as important lessons for our own lives found in the narrative of Avram/Avraham. This guy goes walking and hears a voice that tells him, "Look Avram, go leave this place for your sake... leave your land, leave your birthplace and leave the home of your father ... GO ON, really

LEAVE everything you know and I (the voice) will show you want to do." Based on this experience, our hero, Avram, comes to separate himself from all connections and that he had come to know and to move into what could clearly be called, on many levels, uncharted territory.

Now, imagine when a young adult comes home today and explains to his or her family, friends, and associates that they heard this voice directing them to leave everything they know to follow it and are doing so. This has indeed happened often enough, and parents and family members have been known to consider commitment in a safe place (institution), procuring medication or deprogramming if it is legal and feasible to do so! So, what do we really think about our friend, Avram (or Abraham, as he will come to be known to us)? How do we respond to his adventure in terms of our contemporary standards and conventions? What do we really understand about the scope and magnitude of the challenge he confronted? Further, are there lessons here to be applied to our own lives, so many generations later?

Why was Avram leaving his home and all that he knew and held dear? What was so critically important about this leaving that it is profoundly pivotal in the Western religious world, as Thomas Cahill and many others claim? Is there something archetypal about Avram's journey? We are taught that this story of our shared monotheistic past continues with more promises from God for this special person who accepted all challenges that would be placed before him. Ultimately, he will become the "father of many nations" promised him by God, and this is the point, by the way, at which his name actually becomes Avraham/Abraham. As for the voice which he followed at first and continued to accept as his guide for all that would come, this voice will provide motivation as well as needed support and directions for the actions Avraham would take and decisions he would make, no matter how difficult and challenging circumstances may and will be. Further, this voice will be heard by the generations that will immediately emanate from this Father of Monotheism and will be looked upon for validation by many more generations to come from the respective faith communities that trace their beginnings to this experience and this ultimate risk taker, our father, Avraham.

As one example of this continued legacy, consider the very name of the book written by Khalid Duran (with Abdelwahib Hechiche), which is named <u>Children of Abraham: An Introduction to Islam for Jews</u> (U.S.A.: Ktav Publishing House: 2001), in which we find the following explanation of Muhammad's intentions to return to the mission and experience of Avraham, or Ibrahim for Muslims (8):

> When Muhammad set out on his mission, his intent was not to found a new religion. He was driven by the desire to bring the Peoples of the Book (primarily Jews and Christians) back to the original faith of Abraham… he regarded it as his task to reestablish the original Abrahamic religion …
>
> One who practices *Islam* is a *Muslim*, that is, a person who surrenders to the will of God. According to the Qur'an "It is the cult of your father Abraham." (Sura 22.78).

What was this experience, or as the Sura names it, "cult of Ibrahim?" To what was Abraham surrendering? Abraham takes the huge aptly named leap of faith to follow One and Only One God in a world of multiple deities and begins the process of building a completely new society of accountability to this One and Only One God. Abraham begins with heaps (as well as leaps) of faith, which many believe is later eclipsed by mounds of rules and regulations. Muhammad wants to return to this leap of faith as a foundational expression of the submission that so identifies Islam, as do Jesus of Nazareth and his followers approximately six centuries earlier. What might be looked at as a personal trauma retrospectively becomes a supremely pivotal moment in the history of who we are and who we have become as believers in One and Only One God.

In taking his risk and following the path he does, Avraham represents this entirely new world-view, namely that all we have and are began with The Creator of All, God, to whom we are singularly and exclusively accountable. Herein lay the roots of monotheism as we have come to accept and know it throughout the generations until today, though it must be stated that many will point out that there were shades and hints of such a system in earlier chapters of history. In all of these actions and initiatives in accepting the Oneness of God, Avraham will inaugurate the beginning of the history and legacy of Judaism, Christianity, and Islam. In order to position himself to achieve all of this, there is absolutely no question that Avram took a risk, a big risk! He responded to a challenge that would formulate his mission in life. This resounding response was the most profound indication of his faith, his belief in himself, and certainly his belief in a power bigger and greater than himself. This is a religious response to our world and our place in it! Here we find the rootedness of the exclamation mark that belief in God is for so many people of faith!

What is the message in this archetypal story of a man, a mere mortal, and the risk he takes for his own sake (as well as for our sakes)? What do we learn from the experience of Avram and what we inherit from the motivation that directed, if not guided, him to his destiny? Obviously this action was not without thought or understanding. We must remember that at this time as Avram followed the path set for him, he would not return to his family of birth for celebrations and special occasions. There was no precedent set for him to follow, nor was there a role model to go to for advice, in terms of taking this incredulous step of separation from all that was known and understood to him. Yet as counter- intuitive as this stepping forward was, Avram goes on to become Avraham, the father of many nations. This would be it in terms of his past; once he walked away there was no turning back.

However, Avraham would take the lessons and legacy of his past, those that were positive and those that were difficult, with him as he began to forge a future that would be so very different and seemingly detached from all that he once knew. How do we do this in the context of our own lives both in small ways and in larger ones --- take our past with us into a new and different future? As so many traditions and cultures teach, as well as the science of psychology, the pivotal significance of this rootedness in our past never leaves us. As Madame Chiang Kei Shek is reported to have stated, "We are the sum total of everywhere we have been, everything we have done, and everyone we have known."

We value the past, its teachings and the legacy it bestows upon us. Found in this past are the valuable lessons, important experiences, successes and failures, and so much else that will create the imprint on humanity that each of us can potentially and ultimately achieve in our journey through life. This is the means by which we continue our development, and pass our traditions and practices from generation to generation. In doing so, we use what we have learned and experienced as support and grounding for future challenges and adventures, as new and unfamiliar as they may be. In other words, it is critical to be able to step backwards in order to truly move forward in a meaningful manner.

Consider for a moment that today in our own world, our mental health professionals expend a great deal of time helping people to uncover pasts that can often be forgotten, either consciously or otherwise, in order to be able to move on and create just such a future. This reflects a significant dynamic found in our present reality that is antithetical to the treasuring and knowing of one's past generations and chapters of history as indicated here; namely the fact that many of us have buried, forgotten or walked away from these paths for a wide variety and range of reasons, many of which could be quite legitimate. Nonetheless, we are clearly learning that this is not healthy and that in order to move forward "for our own sakes," we need to know, acknowledge and constructively use what is behind us and therefore with us as well as how to take that legacy and use it in a meaningful manner in the future goals and journey we hope to successfully attain. This is true both for positive as well as negative and painful previous chapters of the collective experience that define our lives.

Let us consider for a moment some experiences that the Midrash and Talmud fill in regarding Avraham's life:

> R. Hiyya the grandson of R. Ada of Yafo said: Terach was an idolater. One day he went out of his shop, and put Avram in charge of selling the idols.
>
> When a man would come who wanted to purchase, Avram would say to him: "How old are you"? The customer would answer: "Fifty or sixty years old". Avram would respond: "Woe to the man who is sixty years old and desires to worship something one day old." The customer would be ashamed and leave.
>
> One day a woman came, carrying in her hand a basket of fine flour. She said: "Here, offer it before them." Avram seized a stick, and smashed all the idols, and placed the stick in the hand of the biggest of them. When his father came home, he asked Avram: "Who did this to my idols"? Avram said, "Would I hide anything from my father? A woman came, carrying in her hand a basket of fine flour. She said: "Here, offer it before them." When I offered it, one god said: "I will eat first," And another said, "No, I will eat first." Then the biggest of them rose up and smashed all the others.

Terach said to Avram: "Are you making fun of me? Do these idols know anything?" Avraham answered: "Do your ears not hear what your mouth is saying?" Terach then took Avraham and handed him over to Nimrod.

Nimrod said to Avraham: "Let us worship the fire". Avraham said to him: "If so, let us worship the water which extinguishes the fire." Nimrod said to him: "Let us worship the water." Avraham said to him: "If so, let us worship the clouds which bear the water." Nimrod said to him: "Let us worship the clouds". Next, Avraham said to him: "If so, let us worship the wind which scatters the clouds." Nimrod said to him: "Let us worship the wind". Avraham said to him: "If so, let us worship man who withstands the wind." Nimrod said to him: "You are speaking nonsense; I only bow to the fire. "I will throw you into it. "Let the God to whom you bow come and save you from it."

Midrash Bereshit Rabbah 38:13

R. Hanan b. Raba further stated in the name of Rab: Avraham our father was imprisoned for ten years, 'three in Kutha, and seven in Kardu.'

Baba Batra 91a (9)

We are taught in our Jewish sources, especially in the Talmud in the Tractate of Berachot, to bless both the good and the bad that occur in our lives. One compelling reason that is given is that even though something may be bad (or hard or difficult) while it is happening, there may be good that comes out of it later. How many times do we hear people in our contemporary world state that a difficult illness or a particularly horrible time in their lives really brought them to a better place? This clearly seems to be within the realm of human reactions to the various occurrences that have the greatest impact on our lives and the trajectory they will assume afterwards.

We remember Avraham for his hospitality and for his concern for others as well as for his ongoing faith in God. Clearly those of us who go through such difficult challenges as those experienced by Avraham learn to be compassionate and caring to others so that they will not suffer as we have. Our suffering can become a teacher, albeit a most difficult and often painful one, as purposeful as it is.

Consider for a moment the contemporary popularity of www.ancestry.com and sites of that type. Our parents, our grandparents and great-grandparents who experienced so many types of "furnaces," be they pogroms, the Holocaust, persecution in other lands and unspeakable hardships too often would not share their stories and their past with us. For that reason, many of us do not know the stories of where we come from, our personal legacy. I personally have tried to find out about my own past from my mother and other members of her generation and without much success due to this code (and perhaps need) of silence. So technology has provided us with a means to recapture and claim this memory. We do exactly that in increasingly significant numbers. When we find these hidden truths of the past, we appreciate our blessings of the present all the more and do not take them for granted. We also learn the names of so many of the Avrahams in our own lives that took their respective leaps of faith, about which no one has spoken to us. We reclaim our past roots, and simultaneously give voice and purpose to the legacies left by those who came before us and helped to bring us to where we are today.

History and past collective experiences are to be valued, cherished and remembered so that we can build upon them, simultaneously reaffirming and changing what we know to be true and real. When we lose and leave them behind completely, we also lose and leave behind their important lessons and with them, sometimes, our very sense of self. So, yes, Avraham left his land, his birthplace and his father's house; but he did not leave the experiences and learned lessons that made Avram Abraham!

He somehow must have intuited this balance between his familiar past and his unknown future, both in terms of how they were connected to each other as well as how they were simultaneously not so inextricably tied together. We learn through the text of Torah, the many classical texts, and commentaries that further explain Avraham's story and his many challenges, he had to walk away from this past and begin anew. However, in doing so, we want to believe that he did not forget the lessons and the learned essentials of his past, both the positive lessons and those that may have been painful. Though he left the idolatry of his generations of ancestors, he would remember this experience and its valuable lessons, as these factors would strengthen his singular resolve to believe in and follow the One and Only One God. He would remember the lessons taught him by his father and the world around him, the challenges he confronted and the history that would always be part of his legacy. This had to be remembered so that his future could be as different from his past *for his sake and good* as well as that of future generations, as they began to forge their collective future!

Questions for Continued Thought and Discussion: As stated in the Introduction, each essay will end with some questions for continued thought. These questions appear within the chapter itself and are intended as a means for you to become part of the conversation begun in these essays.

1. What do you think is the most important lesson and legacy of Avraham's journey for you?

2. Have you been able to maintain the important lessons of your past and the past of your ancestors?

3. What are those lessons?

4. How will you pass them on to the next generations as your legacy?

5. What lessons will you add to this legacy from your experience?

II. Roots and Wings

It is necessary to know from where you come in order to plan where you will go
Popular Saying (attributed to many)

We are taught by our social scientists, philosophers, mental health professionals and so many others that these are the two most important gifts that we can give our children, roots to tie them to their past and the legacy that it holds, and wings to consider new ways in which to experiment with and use that legacy to change our world and help it move forward. One could certainly make the point that it is only through well placed roots that we enable the growth and use of our wings and those of future generations. Yet, in our contemporary society, many others would claim that these two gifts are antithetical to each other and are fearful of either the hold that the past maintains or the uncertainty and lack of guarantee the future promises.

Many submit that these two forces literally pull us in separate directions, threatening our well-being as we feel so torn between these opposing forces. On the other hand, perhaps there is something else we need to consider here as we forge our own philosophy of life and the journeys it has in store for us – that of the balance that comes from equal and simultaneous allegiance and connection to these two opposite pulls, and others that will be presented in this collection of essays. It may very well be that this pull actually keeps us centered and focused on our own journeys, which are inherently rooted in our past as well as driven by the hopes and promise held by the future. The challenge is how we acknowledge this moderate and inclusive approach and its ongoing synergy as well as accept the inherent challenges of balancing the juxtaposition of our roots and wings.

As we have already hinted, one could easily posit the notion that Avraham, our hero from the previous chapter, really did forsake his roots tying him to his land, his birthplace, and his father's house, by using his wings to follow the voice of the One and Only One God. Alternately, we could and perhaps should ask about and consider what was in his background and in the generational experiences to which he was rightful heir that exercised a profound impact upon him and provided him with the ability and motivation to use his wings. Further, to be sure, there may have been lessons and aspects of his past that provided framing for the life that was to come as he left pivotal elements of his past to follow the One God to whom he was completely faithful into an unknown future.

Continuing in the tradition that is now part of our legacy and using the prototype of Avraham's experience as we move forward and closer to our own historical context, we might inquire whether or not our own ancestors and earlier generations forsook their past as they left their lands, the places of their birth and the houses of their parents. Whether they were forced by external forces or internal convictions to leave all that was familiar "for their own sakes" as time passed and events unfolded, we come to acknowledge that in many cases we have far better quality lives as a result of these people who often took such amazing and daunting risks and "followed a voice," whether heard externally or from within.

Yet, it is worthwhile, even necessary, to consider what these ancestors brought from their pasts, namely, the legacies that influenced and predisposed them towards the paths of departure from previously established patterns they would ultimately take. How could they have known which paths of departure they were to take and what legacy they would bring along with them? How did Avraham know? As we have already stated, many people would call that faith, and for Avraham, that faith was clearly invested in the

One and Only One God (his exclamation point, as we have established)!

As we consider our roots and the many generations that came before us, and how we have benefitted from their roots and wings, we now accept our responsibility and consider how we too will pull from the best of that which has gone before us to provide hope and aspirations for that which is yet to come. As our parents and grandparents paved the way for new futures, thus directly providing us with positive benefit and impact, it is now our turn to do the same for our children and the generations that are yet to come. We must all recognize the "roots" and "wings" in our lives as well as the inherent connection and synergy between these two gifts we are each given by virtue of our humanity. This is clearly a product of generational continuity, so valued in every system of thought and living in which the elders teach their children and younger generations the skills, words, literature, prayers and other aspects of a collective legacy that has been gathered by their own previous generations.

Consider for example that every day, the following words appear in the Jewish prayer of the **Shema**, an (many would say the most) important and central prayer to members of the Jewish faith community:

VeShenantam Levanecha

And you shall teach [these words of the Torah] to your children…

The word "*VeShenantam*" is most significant in that it comes from the Hebrew root letters *sh.n.n.,* which mean "to repeat" or "to imprint." The dictate is really to "repeat and/or imprint the words of Torah," not merely to tell or passively "teach" them, rather "to cause them to be learned." So how does one accomplish this much more specific and profoundly invested type of teaching or transmission? Let us seriously think about this, and consider that before one can repeat or imprint words of instruction, one must own and understand these words for oneself. This is quite a concept! It is by recognizing and making the legacy that is our roots our own, that we can engage in the process of using and giving others their wings to go forward.

This truth and valuing of generational teaching is fundamental to Judaism, to other Western religions, to Native American culture and living, and so many other peoples and groups. Besides being valued, generational teaching and the transmission of our past legacy to our future descendants is the very means, the strategy, through which we continue our past through our present and into our future simultaneously encouraging investment and "ownership" of that legacy and using it to build an empowered collective community.

Consider these following explanations of how teachings were imparted, as shared in <u>The Wisdom of the Native Americans,</u> compiled and edited by Kent Nerburn (California: New World Library, 1999):

> Children were taught that true politeness was to be defined in actions rather than in words. They were never allowed to pass between the fire and an older person or a visitor, to speak while others were speaking, or to make fun of a crippled or disfigured person. If a child thoughtlessly tried to do so, a parent, in a quiet voice, immediately set him right. …
>
> Our young people, raised under the old rules of courtesy, never indulged in the present habit of talking incessantly and all at the same time…

In talking to children, the old Lakota would place a hand on the ground and explain: "We sit in the lap of our Mother. From her we, and all living things, come. We shall soon pass, but the place where we now rest will last forever...

Chief Luther Standing Bear, Teton Sioux

No people have better use of their five senses than the children of the wilderness. We could smell as well as hear and see. We could feel and taste as well as we could see and hear....

As a little child, it was instilled into me to be silent and reticent. This was one of the most important traits to form in the character of the Indian. ...

I wished to be a brave man as much as the white boy desires to be a great lawyer or even president of the United States."

Charles Alexander Eastman (Ohiyesa), Santee Sioux (10)

In these words as well as those that come before, between and after them, it is clear to see that the system of education for the Native American is all about doing, learning from and respecting elders, and following by example to the point that the most foundational elements of being a successful and honorable Native American person is inculcated fully into the personality of the child. This is the methodology that truly imprints and causes the other to learn about one's past, while engaging in the process of forging one's future. It is in this manner that the Native American culture is passed through generations, insuring the roots to the past and wings that will carry them into their future.

In the Talmud we see that the value of what is learned as a child is enduring by virtue of it being inculcated by our adult teachers. The repetition of actions and the important modeling that accompanies the teaching are credited for their lasting effect. This is foundational to the purpose of the Oral Law in Jewish Tradition; and the various chains of tradition from generation to generation regarding various practices are repeatedly cited to establish this modeling of dictated traditional living and practice **midor ledor**, from one generation to the next one (11). Rabbinic teachers of the Talmud often reference what they have learned from others and ultimately taken on as their own practices; chains of generations in family units are often cited; and the more generations that are involved in this transmission, the more powerful and accepted the teaching is.

Many of our contemporary writers and thinkers are emphasizing the point that this very effective and invested mode of transmission of legacy and knowledge from generation to generation is clearly at risk at this point in our American society specifically. As a result, the transmission of roots and rootedness and what we have learned from our collective past is seriously compromised. For example, Robert Bly makes this point in his work, The Sibling Society, (U.S.A.: Addison-Wesley Publishing co., 1996). He laments that too many adults and parents have abdicated their roles as the holders and transmitters of past legacies and the guardians of their children's futures, insuring that the younger generation lives a purposeful and safe present. These parents, according to Bly, do not see themselves as the guides in helping their children to make the best informed decisions and act in a responsible way, understanding that to all actions there are attached consequences.

He questions society's dedication to its stake in its future generation, its children as he states as follows:

> The sibling society prizes a state of half-adulthood, in which repression, discipline and the Indo-European, Islamic, Hebraic impulse-control system are jettisoned. The parents regress to become more like children, and the children, through abandonment, are forced to become adults too soon, and never quite make it…
>
> The deepening rage of the unparented is becoming a mark of the sibling society. Of course, some children in our society feel well parents, and there is much adequate parenting; but there is also a new rage…
>
> What the young need – stability, presence, attention, advice, good psychic food, [and] unpolluted stories – is exactly what the sibling society won't give them. (12)

This detachment and disassociation from the past and its experiences and lessons is such a significant part of what keeps psychologists, psychiatrists, and a full cadre of therapists busy in trying to help lost and untended souls "find" themselves, lost because of their own uprooting from their past, whether consciously done or not so. Further, this is characteristic of the very reason that Native Americans would claim that our American family system of transmission, or lack thereof, of past teachings and the very fabric of our lives as a people are at such profound risk of being pervasively endangered, significantly amplifying Bly's painful observation.

To be sure, our social environment and the prominence of peer culture has taken on an entirely new position in our lives since the sixties and the generation gap that threatened the process of generational continuity and transmission of customs and practices and standards that had often defined our previous generations so strongly. Bly's point is that this period of our lives did not only create a break in the continued trajectory of our collective historical memory but also a breakdown in the transmission of all that is foundational to that memory from generation to generation once an entire generation determined that "no one over thirty could be trusted." Herein lie the roots of the "disconnect" that began to grow between parents and children during this window of time about fifty years ago. Bly aptly observes that the parents from this generation too often do not, cannot and will not discipline their children with respect to the very "rites of passage" that they experienced in rejecting their own roots as reflected in the teachings of their own parents.

Simply put, how can our baby boomer adults, asks Bly, who used drugs, drank alcohol, were promiscuous in a variety of ways, and rejected authority so strongly, turn around and guard the generations that may look to them for guidance from the very activities and influences that were their own "rites of passage?" It is in this climate, according to Bly and others, that too many of our children have been left to "bring themselves up" more recently. Many understand all too well that this faulty practice within the human community has dire consequences for the very species that are so socially interdependent and validated within that interdependence by their inherent nature.

It is startling how far we have moved away from our initial valuing and understanding of family in too many instances. As Victor Barnouw comments in his book, <u>An Introduction to Anthropology</u> (United States of America: The Dorsey Press, 1971), regarding the value and importance of the institution of this social unit:

> It is evident that families are quite successful social institutions, despite the fact that they often generate much tension, frustration, and hostility. One reason for the persistence and virtual universality of family groups is that

> children need the close care, attention, and companionship of adults. Families generally provide for these needs more successfully than larger, more impersonal institutions do. Not only is the adult-to-child ratio usually more satisfactory in the family, allowing for better care, but the parents of a child are more likely to feel some personal involvement in him than a hired nurse is apt to do." (13)

The family is extoled by Barnouw for good reason; here is the natural environment for generational transmission. Extended family units such as tribal communities, geographically accessible groupings, such as religious Jewish communities, and other groups where there is a shared investment are indeed powerful and potentially important vehicles of this generational transmission, fulfilling the central role of providing future generations with their roots and their wings. However, when the adult members abdicate this role, clearly the system and its goals fall apart. How interesting that these words were written in 1971, when the roots, if you will, of the problem and challenge presently being discussed and as it exists today, were being so firmly planted!

What do we do and what have we to offer as an antidote in such a cultural context? It is no wonder that it is in response to this very dynamic that we confront at the opposite end of the social spectrum vehement and rigid fundamentalism, where individual choice and informed decision making is not a guided process from generation to generation but rather an imposed and dictated system supervised by those that may be (and too often are) vulnerable to their own tendency towards misuse and abuse of power.

Charles Kimball discusses this phenomenon at length in his book When Religion Becomes Evil (New York: Harper Collins, 2002). He begins this important exploration as follows:

36

> Religion is arguably the most powerful and pervasive force on earth. Throughout history religious ideas and commitments nave inspired individuals and communities of faith to transcend narrow self-interest in pursuit of higher values and truths. The record of history shows that noble acts of love, self-sacrifice, and service to others are frequently rooted in deeply held religious worldviews. At the same time, history clearly shows that religion has often been linked directly to the worst examples of human behavior. It is somewhat trite, but nevertheless sadly true, to say that more wars have been waged, more people killed, and these days more evil perpetrated in the name of religion than by any other institutional force in history. (14)

The very institution of religion that our ethnographers have identified as having the potential to heal and soothe us, having done so for so many generations and millennia, has also been profoundly altered to the point of violence and destruction. Further, many who submit themselves to such monolithic and totalitarian systems and regimens when they have the choice of whether or not to do so (and we freely acknowledge that this is certainly not always the case as in fundamentalist dictatorial regimes with which we are all familiar), may be so inclined as a reaction to the meaninglessness they have confronted in their own lives, void of direction and focus due to a lack of sense of grounding one finds in well placed roots. In short, too many people avoid the choices, empowerment, and options and possibilities of the variegated grey zone found in a moderate, inclusive and thoughtful approach to such choices that includes both one's roots and wings.

The system of *Mitzvot,* commanded actions found in Jewish living and sources, thoughtfully and intentionally followed and continued through the generations is intended to provide just such a balance and system. The truth of the matter is that any observant Jew today is following a system of development that includes not only the statements of Torah, but their interpretations, many discussions of disagreement regarding their meaning and the breadth of their grasp and further development through the generations and resulting different customs through which they are discerned and observed. It is through this ongoing processing that many can insure the intentional application of Jewish law in a manner that provides roots and wings simultaneously, hopefully not being eclipsed by the fundamental extremism of the right or the complete abdication of engagement on the left side of the spectrum of possibilities.

In her book The Trouble with Islam (New York: St. Martin's Press, 2003), Irshad Manji laments the lack of this interpretation in her own Muslim world which is too often evident and plagued by the "herd mentality" that she uses to describe the lack of interpretive, creative and meaningful processing of laws and dictates, where the past holds a noose around the necks of adherents instead of inspiring them to move forward, empowered and enriched. She states as follows:

> ... As for Jews, they're way ahead of the crowd. Jews actually publicize disagreements by surrounding their scriptures with commentaries and incorporating debates into the Talmud itself. By contrast, most Muslims treat the Koran as a document to imitate rather than interpret, suffocating our capacity to think for ourselves. (15)

Certainly, the expression of this rigidity is not a new or novel dynamic, nor is it being presented here as reflective of the absolute entirety of any system of thought or belief. There are well-documented instances of this intransigent definition and extreme, many would say narrow and potentially harmful, use of religious structures throughout the generations of civilization. While often such rigidity may have been motivated by a profound need to maintain identity, in other instances it was unabashedly used to discriminate against others and insure a strong power base for the group employing such a strategy. In fact, fundamentalists in today's world use some of these well-known precedents and models from our past as validation and justification for their own extreme practices as they rebel against what they perceive to be the rampant laxity in principles and standards found too often in our contemporary world, as we have already discussed. To add to the complexity of this dynamic, there are many in our society today who have become rigid anti-religionists for the very reason that history shows us a plethora of instances in which religion was used to destroy and annihilate, not build and heal. It is virtually impossible, for example, to study Western Civilization without focus on wars and destruction in the name of religious righteousness on behalf of this or that church or religious institution.

So now, with what are we left — a society in which there are two compelling and opposite paradigms, one in which there is a ***laissez faire*** attitude in which people "bring themselves up" as Bly explains; and the second according to the thinking of Kimball, in which people abdicate and lose the very sense of self that we as the human species were given as the special gift bestowed upon us by The Creator that distinguishes us from all other created entities in our universe. It is in this climate that many are trying to find their way as reasonable, moderate individuals who are committed to balancing the gifts of religion with the growth and acquired sense of self, the value and need for parenting and the legacy we hold with the hope that we share that our children will become strong adults with a well formulated sense of independence, and of course, the importance and roots of the past with the hopes and the wings of our future.

We learn in ***Pirkei Avot***/ Ethics of the Fathers, 1:14 as follows:

> ***Im Ain Ani Li Mi Li***
> ***U'Kshe'ani Le'atzmi, Mah Ani***

V'Im Lo Achshav, Aimatai

> If I am not for myself, who am I
> If I am only for myself, what am I
> And if not now, when?

This saying, the words of **Hillel the Elder**, a most important Rabbinic teacher during the advent of what we know to be the Common Era, are well known to most, if not all of us. This statement from our Jewish sources teaches us that we must begin with a sense of self for if we are not strong in our own understanding of who we are, then how can we expect others to understand who we are and what our significance is in this world? We also reinforce our learned lesson of balance in this Rabbinic formula for our lives by stating that while we must begin with a sense of self we must also understand and take our place as a member of the group. If we do not and only remain self-centered, who will be there for us? Finally, this balance is to be maintained at all times, beginning with the present. Through our involvement, our activism, our sharing of learned values, and so much else, each one of us has the power and potential to truly exercise an impact on the whole of society. That is to say we become important links in the "chain of tradition" by accepting the lessons of our past, our roots, to use our wings for the benefit of our future, and thus add to the rootedness of our future group members and generations.

As we attempt to find and maintain this balance, we try to integrate the input from different venues that will assist us in accomplishing this goal. For example, we learn from our social scientists that people have basic needs in terms of their developing a healthy sense of personhood. While there are many lists and published treatises that provide us with different aspects of this personhood, for our purposes we will look ever so briefly at four basic human needs that we will consider in our attempt to achieve our sought for balance:

- Need to believe in one self
- Need to belong to a group
- Need to know where one comes from, and
- Need to have an outlet for one's big questions in life

First, one needs to believe in one self and have a good sense of what is important, priorities in the life that will be led, and an understanding of the foundational values that are held to be primary by that person. How do we acquire all of this if not with direction and guidance from those who have already been on this journey longer than us – that is from our collective past, our roots? Further, how do we surround ourselves with people who share these values and priorities? In other words, how do we choose and relate to role models, peer groups and support groups of friends and colleagues?

Let us consider the increasing number of variations of Twelve Step Programs (16), which were developed within a religious context, and their proliferation in our communities – we now have support groups that use this structured and deliberate methodology for those who are addicted to alcohol, food, drugs, sex, gambling, shopping, a variety of inappropriate and dangerous behaviors and so forth. We find increasingly large percentages of our population are experiencing and escaping into these addictive behaviors instead of dealing with the challenges and problems that life presents using the resources of self and already established affinity groups.

Perhaps, this dynamic exists in no small part due to the confusion that the polar opposites described here present and individuals find it harder and harder to "fit in" on either end of this spectrum of extremes, while having misplaced their map of the moderate middle. As these people realize their need to let go of these addictions and engage in the hard work it takes to do so, they come to the realization that they need to surround themselves with people who share their goals and values, look to their own legacies for support if possible, and to acquire and reacquaint themselves with the sense of self that they lost, while accepting the help of a Greater Power (God, perhaps?). Through this process, they will redefine their core identification of self in so many ways.

Secondly, regarding our need to belong, we have often heard the statement, "no man is an island." We are all members of the human family, the species that is known, among other things, for its system of interdependence and social interaction amongst its members. As Hillel states, belonging to a group is important in that, among other things, it validates and provides a further sense of purpose for self. If one is only alone and remains alone, then what is that person … to others as well as to self? So, if group identification is such an important and primary human need, we must have available options for belonging to and engaging in such groups. We are accountable in insuring that there are reasonable choices for such membership across our ideological, religious, socio-economic, political, gender, sexuality and other spectrums for all of us who need such support.

Within the Orthodox Jewish community, it is a known phenomenon that many products of other ideological communities, for example specifically identified "success stories" of the Conservative Jewish movement, have come to align themselves within these more religiously observant groupings due to a lack of options within the very communal context in which these people grew and matured in a window of time approximately thirty to forty five years ago, which has basically, for lack of a better set of words, "moved to the left." Simply put, individual adherents were taught and guided in a life of religious observance and practice that too often could not be found within the community with which they are most familiar and they were then put in the position in which they had to find a different affinity group. The "moderate middle" groups are the entities that often suffer the most in this movement towards the polar opposites that our contemporary society seems to favor too often. In this situation, where many get their "roots" and where their resulting "wings" will take them may have to be different support structures.

Conversely, there are those who were raised within certain elements of the Orthodox community who have lived a rather separate, highly regulated and dictated life with little if any input from or exposure to anything outside of this regimented existence. As time moved on, some members of this community reacted to what was perceived as the "pull to the right" and felt excessively weighted down by the pull of their roots and wanted to grow and use their wings. In other words, the balance indicated in the pull of and response to both of these factors, roots as well as wings, was not found in their communities or groups of origin.

Unfortunately, too often many members of our faith communities cannot find validation for this balance of their roots and their wings and the synthesis of their interaction. In these cases, too often, individuals will run as far as possible from all that is familiar to them and we are left with the question of whether or not this is "for their sake or for good." For all of those who can find new communities of affinity that embrace and value them, there are others who cannot find an alternative community and structure into which they fit and often end up feeling and being further isolated and lost. For example, in Israel there has been the popping up of organizations that run halfway house type programs as a haven for these young as well as older adults who run from their religious communities and have nowhere else to go.

Similar dynamics have been observed in other communities of faith as well. What does this say about our larger faith communities and their own definition of self and the individuals that will be drawn to such a collective definition? How well are we doing (or not doing) in helping our community members to maintain their own needed balance of self and group, roots and wings? As the Fundamentalists pull to the right and the Secularists pull to the left in many of our religious and faith communities, what *groups* remain as viable options for those individuals left in the middle of the continuum of options? This too has been the subject of many of our contemporary social scientists and concerned observers as we look ahead. Often we have many more questions regarding an uncertain future than clear answers that tie our roots of the past to our wings for the future.

Another example of this need for group affiliation has been observed in our general societal framework. Note that the "bar scene" has changed remarkably during the last few decades and that singles as well as couples are now choosing different options for "groups" to join than previous generations had chosen. Consider the plethora of on line communities and affinity groups, the glaring public eye on reality television, interest groups created by shared hobbies, professional affiliations and more. The problem is that the availability of so many more options has not relieved the challenge of too many of our contemporary societal members who continue to feel too much alienation.

Churches, synagogues, mosques and other religious centers are working hard as they weigh in with their options, often fueling the development of constituencies and affinity groups quite different from those traditionally associated with these venues. In short, we are all being challenged by new definitions of self and the groups that all of these individual selves compose. One noted dynamic in this development is that in a significant number of instances those who had previously left the religious centers that were familiar to them have created these new entities. They had discerned that the purely social options that they had embraced earlier became devoid of the foundational values, that is, the roots that they hold dear. In other words, from an external objective perch, it might appear that in the absence of balance, necessity has recreated it in both familiar and new venues, allowing for roots to be nourished and wings to grow.

This is not dissimilar to many families of the fifties, the sixties and the seventies who reared their children in a value laden environment and then these children who are now adults searched for groups in which these values may not have been quite so present, only to return to them later. In this return, many of these rebellious younger adults have become deeply religious mature adults. While we examine so many forms of mobility – social, religious, political, and economic – in our contemporary reality, we are also confronting a type of group value mobility that acts as an overlay for these other dynamics. Individuals use different criteria to find their affinity groups and the choices themselves help to create the new alternatives. Everyone needs to belong somewhere and we are pulling out all of the stops, one way or another!

Thirdly, we have already addressed the importance of our rootedness in the past and the critical need we have for understanding this story of our beginnings. For those of us for whom this past is positive and filled with what are considered to be "warm fuzzy memories" we can depend and pull on that past for our values, our sense of self, and guidance in determination of what groups we will join. However, a word must be devoted to those of us who come from what mental health professionals have defined as "toxic pasts." Many have had to break away from established patterns of abuse, substance dependency, and dishonest and destructive behaviors and so much else. In such instances, those who break away have to look elsewhere for validation of what has become their own internalized system of values and standards.

For these individuals, finding new groups with which to identify is critically important as they are trying to "**re-root**" themselves before using their wings. Further, as stated earlier, this is done as those who are seeking to "re-root" themselves determine what constructive parts of their past lives can be brought along into their new existence, in the manner that Avraham did (as we explored in Chapter One). This is one of the many important roles that the various support groups that have become such a familiar sight in the landscape of our society play. While Avraham had no such support group to help him through his own significant transition, today this journey need not be a lonely nor a solitary one as it must have been for our hero and so many others so long (and not so long) ago.

Religious Jewish families and communities who have maintained their rooted lifestyle for generations have confronted the newly religious members of their community, the ***Ba'alei Teshuvah*** (roughly meaning those who seek and find answers, thus returning to their roots), who are on such journeys. One of the trends is that some of these newly observant Jews, in their re-rooting process, have too often turned away from their pasts -- and all that is part of it, both "good" and "not so good" -- for a variety of reasons and are sometimes very needy in their approach to and involvement in their new groups and lifestyles. There is often a powerful and visceral sense of responsibility to help these people regain a sense of self in their re-rooting process. It is sometimes observed that these people have a tendency to go a bit overboard in their new religious fervor and may have to be tempered. There actually is a preferred methodology of teaching "one mitzvah at a time" so as to avoid this sensory and personal overload. Clearly this is a challenge for our Christian and Muslim communities as well as other faith groupings. Think of the phenomenon of ***Born Again Christians*** and the charismatic influence of such groups in our larger American landscape as yet another clear example of this dynamic.

Perhaps, we can return once again to our friend, Avraham, for an important lesson here. Note should be taken that his name was ultimately changed from his given name of Avram in recognition of

46

the meaning and significance of his past joined with his hopes for his future and that of future generations that would come from his roots. He moved from his past of idol worship and behaviors that would no longer be part of his reality once he followed the voice of God. Yet there was some baggage from his past that would clearly continue to serve an important purpose in terms of the journey he was to take. He did not summarily dismiss all of his "roots" but took those that were appropriate as he began to use his wings. Herein lays a formula for all of us to consider, including those discussed above. There will be some aspects of our past history that will help us in our future, whichever direction it takes us. We should remember and treasure this truth, with respect to ourselves, and our own development of self, as well as in our interactions with others. In other words, we must remember to NOT "throw the baby out with the bathwater" as we consider the integration of our past with the future part of our life journeys. As an example, consider that many people who decide to become more religious in their lives come from homes with conservative values, if not religiously or ritualistically observant lifestyles. They are then predisposed to find that affinity group that most validates and represents the values that they have incorporated as their core identifying principles. Where does one find such a community? This is often the attraction of these individuals to the religious lifestyle and the community in which it is activated.

Finally, it cannot be emphasized enough that we must have an outlet for those really important and critical questions that we are so compelled to often ask but seldom find the definitive answers that satisfy them, if in fact such even exist. These questions are often representative of the most painful corners of our souls and it may be comfort we seek, that is, approaches to our painful and questioning corners more than answers that are definitive and more often than not, less than appropriate for the seeker! Maimonides, Ecclesiastes/Kohelet, and other commentators and sources warn us repeatedly that the answers would be too painful for us and we would not even have the strength and the inner fortitude to discern them were we to be able to "reach" them. It has often been said that it is the journey, not the destination that defines us and is most important in our lives. We will do better to acknowledge that it is this journey and its questions that we will use to develop approaches to the challenges that will always be present in our lives. Further, in doing so, we will need to accept that we will most likely not find "the one and only answer" to any of our questions! Perhaps, then we have the best chance to continue to develop as healthy and well-balanced thinking beings in the process of becoming all that we will be!

Further, when thinking in terms of approaches and options, we must acknowledge that different people will be drawn to different approaches and that these variations can potentially be equally valid, given the circumstances of each person's journey. While we travel as groups, with our roots and wings intact, we must come to the place where we all realize that there are individual aspects to each person's journey that will inform the individual approaches we each take in our lives.

I remember finding this message illustrated decades ago in one of Steven Spielberg's earlier films that achieved critical acclaim, ***Close Encounters of the Third Kind.*** The journey depicted in this film was so representative of this notion. There is a "message" that appears, of which people are not sure of its meaning in terms of content or source. People are drawn to the "message," and as the involvement becomes more intense, what began as group journeys become very individuated as individuals are drawn in different ways and for various reasons to the same stimulus.

What is a totally appropriate and positive approach for one person will not necessarily be the same for someone else. Here we must recognize and appreciate that we have individuated needs to be met and paths to follow. If we can learn to think of options to follow being many as opposed to the one and only one way to go, chances are greater that our roots and wings will both continue to have their proper place in our lives.

Given these basic human needs of understanding self, belonging to a group, having a sense of where we come from and a place for our big questions; if the direction and guidance that is fundamentally needed is not provided for people, they will seek it elsewhere. This dynamic is the topic of much study as we are looking at the phenomenon of those members of our society who "check out" from what should be their increasing sense of responsibility, the numbers of dysfunctional adults who don't seem to be able to "grow themselves up" at increasingly older ages, and those about whom we have already spoken who have sought out alternative means of belonging and validation. Bly's <u>The Sibling Society</u> articulates the problem of a society that is too often devoid of the generational transmission that insures our wings and roots remain connected, bolstering and validating each other, while responding to these most basic personal needs.

As we have seen, we human beings are inherently and naturally connected to our past, and to the conventions that unite us as members of our human family and the various subgroups to which we belong as members of this family. Further, we have aspirations that reflect our hopes for something better and more evolved, both as members of the groups of which we are part and as individuals who will take chances to make life better and more meaningful for ourselves and others to whom we are bound in so many different ways. Thus, as natural as our roots and wings are to us, so it is our task to find a way to come to terms with each so that there is mutual benefit and balance within and among these two pulls on our lives, so that they are complementary and not antithetical to one another.

Questions for Continued Thought and Discussion:

1. What are the roots from your past that are most significant to you and from where do they come?

2. What are your most profound hopes for the future, that is, the wings you want to grow?

3. How do you see that your wings are a product of your roots?

4. What roots will you want to give others (e.g. your children, grandchildren) as they forge their own future?

5. How will these roots that you pass on be the same as those that you have from your past?

6. How will these roots that you give to other be different from those of your past and why?

III. Free Choice or Informed Choice?

And God said, we will make the human being in our image, in our likeness.
And God created the human being in God's image

Genesis, chapter 1, verses 26 - 27

FREE CHOICE is a most important concept that so many writers, people of faith, philosophers and others have tried to unravel and discern for as many generations as such discourse has been around. It is so valued philosophically and practically, especially in our Western society. Yet, there are many other nations and groupings both throughout history and in our contemporary world in which this most important quality is much more myth than reality, if even that. In Fundamentalist and Totalitarian regimes, FREE CHOICE is a, if not the most formidable enemy, as it will threaten the very fabric of such regimes, so dependent on the "herd mentality" that Irshad Manji speaks about in her book.

Perhaps one of the greatest ironies of all is how fundamentalist regimes will "give their people the choice" to validate their control and abdicate their own right to choose and then choose to do so. I know that may feel a bit unwieldy but read that sentence again if you need to. As Anuradha Ketaria explains in her book, <u>Democracy on Trial: All Rise</u> (United States of America: Algora Publishing, 2011),

> While free to choose, people have often voted for fundamentalist parties over reforming ones in the developing world. This has puzzled intellectuals who believe that democracy is the instrument that would deliver these societies from their backwardness. Helen Keller once said,

"The heresy of one age becomes the orthodoxy of the next." (17)

In fact it has been posited by more than a few academic observers that it is this one capacity of free choice of the individual that totalitarian and fundamentalist governments most loathe about Western countries, and the most compelling element that causes reference to the United States as "the Big Satan" in the media and various forms of publicity sponsored by such governments and related organizations. After all, if people actualize this element of their being, would this not threaten the forced opaque unity and compliance that is critical for a dictator to maintain absolute rule and power? Upon considering the larger picture, surely we understand how FREE CHOICE can be seen by some as a given of life that spurs one on to great things while others see it as the most vile element possible to be squashed totally!

So, let's try to unravel what free choice really is, if this is even possible. The first question is do we human beings truly have unfettered and completely free choice? Let's begin our consideration of this question by looking at the text above. In the beginning of the Torah, we are told that after God had carefully crafted and created the various components of our universe, God took even more time and so purposely thought about and considered ever so carefully the creation of the human being. God did not simply "say and do" as was the case with other components of the story of Creation as indicated in Chapter One of the Torah. Rather, God looked around and stated that human beings should be created and these human beings should be significantly more developed than all other components of Creation, which God had also fashioned.

Commentators and those who study this text point out that one should consider the possibility that God thinks that this is so important that God actually consults others in this process. Various possibilities that are proposed as being God's collaborators in this profound undertaking of the specific fashioning of the human being include the angels of God's heavenly court, all of the created beings up to this point, and even the human being, through the steps of its own Creation. According to the Vilna Gaon, an eighteenth century commentator, we could include all of the above as involved participants in this singularly elevated process. Regardless of which of these or other presented options one accepts, the point is clear that the creation of the human being was wholly different, the essence of this being was wholly different and the ability to consciously and intentionally choose and determine is at the core of this wholly different existence as described in this early reference in the Torah and several that will follow.

Notice that a bit later in Chapter Two of Genesis, verse seven, we read as follows:

> And HaShem God formed the human being with dust from the earth;
> And God blew into the human's nose the breath of life;
> And the human became a living soul.

Here we see that there is a part of the human that is fashioned from the lower realms of the earth on which we reside and of which we are part. In fact, one must note that the very word for person – **adam** – is the same word/root for earth – **adamah** – in Hebrew. Additionally, we see that another part of the human is fashioned from the higher realms of our Universe, with God's direct input clearly stated as blowing the essence into the earthly being that gives that being a soul. This tradition of understanding the creation of the human is given to us by Ramban and cited and expanded by many others, in their attempts to get as close as possible to understanding what we cannot totally discern.

Many look at this as a rather simple formula in which our body is of the earth and our soul is of God. Yet, we must also consider that it is at this very point, according to some of our scholars and students of Torah, that God and the human being that has been fashioned become partners in the maintenance and growth of all that was created. This shared partnership is symbolized in a foundational manner by the very breath that man breathes, as a result of God's initiative. This acquired breath of life could be looked at as our very essence and thus informs how we choose within the context of our collaborative relationship with God. It is this very attribute that differentiates the human being from all other created beings in Creation.

Gerald L. Schroeder, Ph.D. pursues this significant possibility in his book Genesis and the Big Bang (New York: Bantam Books, 1990) in which he references the work of Nachmanides (Ramban) and his commentary in which Ramban states that it is at this point in Chapter Two where the human being receives the soul that is ordained for him by God, while in the earlier statements of the human's creation in Chapter One, we come to an understanding of how we received our form and capabilities to be and function, the more tangible aspects of being human, if you will.

He states as follows:

> The specialty of mankind is not the physical attributes we have. All primates have grasping upper limbs and overlapping binocular vision … The size of the cranial cavity, from which brain size is estimated, has not changed much in the primate we call *Homo sapiens* for the past 100,000 years…
>
> All animals received a life-giving spirit, a *nefesh* in Hebrew. The animal that was to become Adam was no exception.

> However, into the physical form that contained the *nefesh* of Adam, the Creator placed an additional spirit, of soul, the *neshamah*. It is this that has set mankind apart from the other animals …
>
> Nachmanides … indicates that reasoning, speech, and all the other capabilities of mankind … are subject to the spirit that was given to mankind alone … by God (18)

Perhaps, then according to the earlier reading in which what man receives from the upper and lower realms is clearly divided, one option is that we could posit that our capacity for FREE CHOICE comes from the inherent quality of our being human and we no longer have to look to God for an explanation of what might have "gone wrong" with respect to our use of this capacity. But, this is too often regarded as a problematic option, as the tangible (visual and touchable) features of the human are attributed to the earthly part of who we are while the soul encompasses those capacities and abilities we feel and are motivated by, though we cannot reduce them to tangible form.

Here is the greatest and most difficult irony, namely, that which makes us most human as well as singularly different from all other created beings and all that entails is precisely what we cannot quantify or accurately define. Working through the problem and challenge of reconciling the good gift God has bestowed upon the human to choose (and reason, as indicated above) and the human's choice to use it poorly still remains to be resolved or at least addressed by a set of approaches that may or may not work for us. How we perceive and resolve this dilemma in our own lives will say much about each of us as individuals and our approach to as well as role in the world, the stage we all share with our different and various orientations and approaches. Further as noted above, great care must be taken so we do not abdicate this capacity to choose for others in the name of choice itself!

The exact elements of this significant difference that so defines the human being have been the subject of many philosophies and thought systems throughout our civilized history. We are taught in Jewish thinking that at the point as described in Chapter Two, Verse Seven of Genesis, the human is created with two dispositions or initiatives, one called *yetzer tov* is our initiative for and to do good, while our *yetzer hara* is our initiative for and to do what may not be for our good (or for our sake!). Further complicating these two conflicting modes is the third element we are given, namely **Bechirah chofshit** or the freedom of choice in how and when to use each of these initiatives.

On one hand, FREE CHOICE is foundational to use of our wings that we are given to take us forward and sometimes further away from our roots. This is exactly one of the profound tensions that Anuradha Ketaria explores in her treatise on the intentions versus the challenges and results of democracy.

Thomas Cahill makes this point in a different context in his discussion in The Gifts of the Jews, when he talks about Abraham's choice to go and make a decision that would release him from the well-established patterns of mankind and the previous generations that repeated well-worn paths within the established circle of existence. The very choice to follow a different direction and the potential and profound difference this point of departure could and would make in the coming generations of the story of civilized and religious man must be seen as pivotal, as we have already established.

Further, as stated earlier, we have often experienced the significance of such points of departure due to human initiative more personally in terms of the choices made by our own previous generations with respect to our families and the new life that we were enabled to explore and ultimately experience.

So this critically important and defining feature of free choice is a good thing. In fact, it is a great thing that characterizes the breadth and wonder (as well as the breath that was breathed into the human) of the core of our humanity! The challenging and difficult part of this equation is that this is true both in terms of the constructive and positive uses of our capacity to choose as well as instances where such choices can produce horrible, even catastrophic, results. Both options are necessarily required parts of this package deal. In fact, when we return to our consideration of how many view religion in a negative light due to the many painful chapters of history in which the institution of religion was used to destroy and break down, this is all about the use of choice in the name of religion and beliefs that are informed by it.

Free choice is a capacity that was bestowed upon all human beings by God according to Jewish thinking and sources. So, as many think, if God gave this gift to the human being and it is a good gift, or more precisely, a gift that can be used for good and noble purposes, then is God not responsible and culpable when the human being God created uses the gift of choice for evil purpose and gain? This is precisely the question that is posed by Harold Kushner in his book, When Bad Things Happen to Good People and so many other writers and thinkers. How could this possibly not be so or how could we think otherwise regarding The One Who Ordains All To Be? This is exactly the type of theological reasoning that leads to questions such as "Where was God during the Holocaust?" or "How can one act on behalf of God and strive for as well as achieve evil purposes in the name of God?" Such is the question that is often posed regarding extreme Fundamentalists who will use terror and a variety of harmful measures to achieve what they consider to be noble religious purposes according to the choices that they make, including torture and even desired annihilation of other peoples.

It should be noted that we read about God's own rethinking about the parameters of free choice and the potential regret that God has regarding the pulls on that process in the Talmud as follows:

> R. Chana Bar Acha said: There are four things that God regrets having created: Exile, the Chaldeans, the Yishmaelites, and the Evil Inclination/ ***yetzer hara***. (Sukkah 52b)

Looking around us today, one could well understand this regret on a human scale. However, to attribute regret to God is clearly problematic for many, for we teach elsewhere that every single thing that God created has a purpose and a role to fulfill. So too it is with the creation of free choice and the two oppositional pulls that vie for its attention.

Clearly, there is a profound sense of responsibility that must accompany this privilege and capacity for free choice, especially when it is used for the purpose of behaving, as God would want us to do. We as the individuals that have been given free choice must also understand and accept the accountability that comes with the gift we have been given. Let's for a moment consider what our reality would be regarding this choice if God did "fix" the misinformed and disastrous choices people continually make. If God were to "throw out the net" and catch us every time we use this capacity inappropriately, then the gift we had been given would be meaningless! So God cannot correct our poor choices each time. God cannot protect us from choosing to choose poorly. If God did so, then it would not by definition be FREE choice that characterizes our humanity so profoundly and pervasively!

Our Jewish texts even entertain the notion that eradicating "our choosing to choose poorly" or using our *yetzer hara* would solve the problem. However, the point is repeatedly reinforced that this *yetzer hara* is also the creative urge in us and we need it, used properly. In Genesis Rabbah 9:9, we are taught that if it were not for this creative urge that inspires us to achieve and improve, we would not work, build or create anything to change our world. In Yoma 69b, we learn about the desire to destroy the *yetzer hara*. After three days of its absence, it was discovered that no one could even find a single egg, for sustenance. Why? Because if nothing was missing or lacking and everyone was acting in a positive way, then why would there be a need to create anything new, even an egg? Clearly, this urge to create anew and fill in something that is not there yet is needed in the human equation of our world to improve and make it better; what is critical is how we use it appropriately.

In an ideal situation, there is a simple set of statements of equation that would appeal to our sense of reason and can basically be formulated as follows:

- Good choices chosen well will produce good results.
- Poor choices chosen poorly will produce poor results.

Obviously, we know all too well that this is NOT how our life and capacity for choosing goes. We live in a real world that is tainted by the reality that an ideal is just that – an ideal, but not the reality that defines and impacts upon our lives. Especially in our post 9/11 world, we are constantly reminded of the horrible ramifications for so many when other people can choose poorly according to one's code of good and bad, and that these choices can and do produce what those who have chosen consider to be good results. Further, people can choose well, namely to go to work daily to provide responsibly for their family and to be productive members of society and suffer from the tragic and horrific results of such choices of others in the very places in which good people are fulfilling their responsibilities.

In such instances, the wires are crossed between one's actions and intentions, and the results that impact upon another. In these cases, it may very well be that the statements above need to be amended as follows:

- While we hope that good choices will produce good results, we acknowledge that they will sometimes produce poor results for the best-intentioned individual.
- While we hope that poor choices will produce poor results, they will sometimes produce favorable or good results for the perpetrator at the expense of others.

Further, we must be mindful that when wires are crossed, what one person considers to be "good results" from their actions and choices could in fact be horrible and tragic results for another in the impact of said choices and actions. How do we interface such disparate views and perceptions in our world, not just intellectually, but practically when it is our lives that are so affected by this juxtaposition of motivations and understanding?

In all of our philosophizing and analyzing, and thinking and processing that has become once again part of our daily reality, as was and is the case in our post-Holocaust Jewish community and civilized world and in so many other instances in our history, we have a most difficult time reconciling our use of our free choice and God's pulling back to allow us to use this gift that so defines us as thinking humans and yet can produce such catastrophic results. Simply, to put a spin on Harold Kushner's paradigm of questions from When Bad Things Happen to Good People (U.S.A.: Schocken Books, 1981), how can we come to terms with God's inherent and rooted goodness, while at the same time understanding that the good gift of free choice which God gave to man can be used for evil purposes? If man can do and be evil, how can The Creator of man who created such people be wholly good? (19)

Obviously, this dilemma and its myriad of corollary issues are far from simple and clear. In fact, there is a point early on in the story of **Bereshit**/ Genesis when God observes how this capacity of choice has been used in generations of human history for purposes other than God had perhaps hoped and intended. As reflected earlier, it is here that God actually regrets having bestowed this gift upon the humans God so carefully crafted, which is, to be sure, a rather overwhelming concept to absorb.

We read about this regret as well, regarding the very creation of the human being, in the earliest chapters of the Torah:

> God saw how great man's wickedness was on earth,
> And how every plan devised by God's mind was nothing but evil all the time.
> And God regretted that God had made man on earth,
> And God's heart was saddened.
> God then said, "I will blot out from the earth the men whom I created…for I regret that I made them.
>
> Genesis Chapter 6, verses 5 - 7

For many reasons that should seem apparent, this is a very troubling text. The commentaries differ on how we are to understand it, but within these variations is a common thread that God conveys great sadness and regret while some also look at man's angst and conflict regarding this gift of choice. Rashi, our well-known medieval commentator, goes so far as to suggest that God is so profoundly distraught that God lets go of God's most powerful standard of compassion and instead seeks justice as resolution for man's horrible failure, and perhaps, thus, God's failure as well. What a powerful idea it is that God may have regretted fashioning the human with this gift of choice while the human may have preferred not to have this very gift that so defined the nature of humanity! Rashi presents the notion that it is at this point that God and man come to certain realizations about each other and their respective realms as well as the limitations EACH must exercise regarding the realm of the other.

Ultimately God will not be able to control man and how man uses the gifts bestowed upon him by God; and for his part, man will not come to know and understand all about God. It is now ever so clear that there will always be a wall between them no matter how close God and the being God created come together. We will come to the realization, as **Moshe Rabbeinu** comes to discern at the Burning Bush and others will continually reaffirm, that God and humanity will not walk together in the fullest and most satisfying and obvious sense. The question is whether this harsh realization is ultimately one of discord, resignation or comfort in coming to understand certain realities and limitations of the human species and their interfacing with The Creator. Further, what will we choose to do with this realization and how will we actualize it in our lives?

Harold Kushner teaches us how through choosing to show concern for each other and be invested in our collective reality, "human beings are the language of God." Herein lays a wonderful challenge and validation of the initiative we can take in our lives in becoming the person that can "walk with God." We "walk" in the initiatives we take that model the actions that God wants us to use in our lives.

Notice this teaching from the Talmud regarding how we can resolve this seeming obstacle in our lives as found in Sotah 14a:

> R. Hama son of R. Hanina further said: What does the text mean: "You shall walk after (or with) God" (Deuteronomy

13)? Is it, then, possible for a human being to walk after God; for has it not been said: "For God is a devouring fire" (Deuteronomy 4)? But the meaning is to walk after the attributes of the Holy One. Just as God clothes the naked, as it says, "And God made garments of skins for Adam and his wife, and clothed them" (Genesis 3), so do you also clothe the naked. The Holy One, blessed be God, visited the sick, for it is written: "And God appeared to Avram by the oaks of Mamre" (Genesis 18), so do you also visit the sick. The Holy One, blessed be God, comforted mourners, for it is written: "And it came to pass after the death of Abraham, that God blessed Isaac his son" (Genesis 25), so do you also comfort mourners. The Holy one, blessed be God, buried the dead, for it is written: "And God buried Moshe in the valley" (Deuteronomy 34), so do you also bury the dead.

Source: Adapted from Soncino translation

Similarly we find this sentiment reinforced in other religious traditions, seeking the same type of unity and peaceful shared experience. Consider this quote from a sermon delivered by J.C. Philpot (1802 – 1869), a preacher who resigned from the Church of England in 1835 and became a Baptist. This excerpt is from his words on Sunday, January 23, 1859 as preached at North Street Chapel.

"Can two walk together, except they be agreed?" Amos 3:3

> The Lord here, under the form of a question, enunciates a very important and pregnant truth. "Can two walk together," he asks, "except they be agreed?" What must be the inevitable reply? Surely not! Unless agreed in heart, how can they walk together in person? But do we see this agreement as a substantial fact, or as a general case? Look at man and

his brother man. Take men as they exist in this present world. Can we say that they are agreed, or, that being agreed, they walk together? The very physical features of the world, in its original formation as well as present constitution, widely separate man from man. What lofty mountains, deep rivers, wide seas, and barren tracts, naturally, *physically* sever men asunder! But these natural barriers of division are as nothing compared with the way in which man is separated *morally* from man. (20)

So, we are being cajoled to take important initiatives to help and share with each other. In fact, in the Talmud we are told that God actually showed us how to do this through God's own actions of kindness and compassion. Further, by walking with God through our intentional actions, we are also connecting and walking with our fellow humans, in the way that God intended. Then Philpot, for his part, shows that just as we have to find a way for man and God to walk together in a way that acknowledges the limits and differences of each, we are likewise challenged in our attempts to walk with each other. All of this involves using our capacity to choose to walk with the other in the ways that are available to us.

Aside from the religious ramifications of this difficult reality, we cannot resist the temptation to ask where did things begin to "go wrong" in terms of this sense of shared interaction with God and with each other. Upon returning to our story in the earliest chapters of **Bereshit**/Genesis, we read as follows within the narrative of the Garden of Eden, the paradise in which God "placed" the humans, now identified as male and female, to live:

> HaShem/God took the human and placed the human in the Garden of Eden to work it and to guard it. And HaShem God commanded the human saying, "From every tree of the

> garden you may eat. And from the Tree of Knowledge of Good and Bad, you must not eat from it, for on the day that you eat from it, you will surely die."

Genesis, Chapter 2, verses 15 - 17

Here specific and clear instructions are given to the human beings regarding what is available for the use of the human and what is not as well as the consequences of not following the explicit directions as indicated. However, through the very nature of the process of Creation, the capacity to choose whether or not to abide by these instructions indicated by the Creator was also given. The interfacing of this human capacity to choose and the circumstances in which such choices are to be made will continue to challenge all of us.

As our story from Genesis moves on, we see how this element of choice will unfold in the Garden of Eden narrative as narrated in Chapter 3: 1 - 5:

> And the serpent was cunning more than all of the animals of the field that HaShem God had made. The serpent said to the woman, "Perhaps God said you should not eat from any tree of the garden, God said "You shall not eat from it, and you shall not touch it or you will die." And the serpent said to the woman, "You will surely not die, for God knows that on the day that you eat from it, your eyes will be opened and you will be as God in knowing good and bad."

Ramban (Nachmanides) explains that the element of desire can be found here and this is the element that makes the process of choosing wholly different for humans as distinguished from God. God can and will choose well and appropriately because according to Ramban, basically there are no ulterior motives, no other mitigating factors that would taint or influence God's choice. For the human being, however, coming from the ground and possessing tangible features and attributes, this species is aware of potential tangible gains and how good they feel. Therefore desire and "what one wants to do" factors into the choosing that one does, or does not, do. Now, when looking at the text from Sotah 14a and the words of J.C. Philpot, we can begin to discern what went "wrong" even though this is such a fundamental element of what it means to be the human beings we are.

Our Jewish sages teach us that the more God gives, the more God still has to give. By contrast, when a human gives a gift that is tangible, he has less that is tangible. So we must address the role of self-interest in the choices we make, namely what is the other person receiving in our interaction; what is my benefit? By clothing the ones who need clothes, we give resources. By visiting the sick and burying the dead, we share our time. For Philpot, by acknowledging that I do not have to agree with you, I may be sacrificing ego or hubris. Do I *desire* to do these things, to yield to others in a manner that will potentially "lessen" my resources, my time, or my status? Now, let's consider the choices we make within this context!

Regarding this conflict, we read in the book of **Melachim I**/ Kings I that King Solomon, known for his wisdom and so much else, had a dream in which God came to him and asked him what he wanted as a gift from God. We read as follows as Solomon indicates what he has chosen as what he wishes to receive from God among the options that were offered:

> May you, God, grant your servant an understanding heart to judge your nation, to understand between good and bad, because who is able to judge your difficult people?
>
> Kings I, Chapter 3, verse 9

Here we read of a great king who will be known both in Jewish history for his greatness as a ruler of the Jewish nation, and by the world for his unsurpassed wisdom. To be sure, he will acquire great riches and tangible results throughout the history and growth of his kingdom for which he will be known as well. Nonetheless, notice the gift that he has chosen for God to give him, that of wisdom and ability to judge the people whom have been entrusted to his care. It is important to consider what this does teach us about choices that all of us can and do make. We know well that King Solomon will achieve his place in history due in no small part to this very correct and appropriate choice, and in spite of choices he will later make that will not be equally so, and certainly not as motivated by intrinsic good. Further, as tradition has it, he will come to question and doubt his own choices and their value later in his life, as well as the purpose of choosing altogether in the writings ascribed to him in the book of Kohelet/Ecclesiastes.

For now, let us return to our earlier story of the Garden of Eden. Regardless of the religious traditions and beliefs in which we individually find ourselves rooted, chances are that we all know how this narrative continues to progress. The human beings were in fact thrown out of their paradise for choosing to go against the very instructions provided by God. Supposedly, they, unlike, King Solomon, in the story above, did not choose "correctly." Although like so much else, this is not quite that simple. Perhaps they did make exactly the appropriate choice to go against God, reinforcing the point that how one uses FREE CHOICE to CHOOSE FREELY and not automatically do what is predetermined to be correct.

Now, it should and must be indicated that the commentators look at the continued story of Creation itself to make the point that God spoke to the man and it was actually the woman who instigated this sequence of events of listening to the serpent, eating from the forbidden tree, and ultimately being expelled from the Garden.

However, upon looking even more closely at our story, there is a much more complex problem here. It was in fact the lowly serpent of the ground that began this downward spiral of poor choosing and the results. So, if God created all and if this poor choice that produced such catastrophic events emanated from the actions of the serpent, then is God, the Creator responsible and is what happened exactly what God intended to be the result? In such a case, what role can we actually attribute to free choice in the lives of the human beings, if any at all?

How can we even consider the possibility of disassociating God The Creator who has placed all elements in the universe from the actions and consequences of the actions of those created beings for whom God is responsible? Looking at how these events ultimately unfold, we cannot help but wonder if this was a type of set up. After all, God is constantly testing the human beings whom God so carefully and deliberately created throughout the Torah and according to the beliefs of so many different people of faith, throughout our history and its many generations, continuing through today and into the future. This is God's prerogative, so what does this throw into our already rather complex mix of ideas and questions we are developing here? Now, what is the place of free choice and man's ability to exercise use of this aspect of his being, if in fact God is in any way "pulling the strings," so to speak?

After all of this consideration, we realize that we have more questions at this point than we did earlier. It is within this context that we return to the idea and question of to what degree do we really in fact have the gifted quality of free choice? Maybe we need to reframe our thinking a bit. What if we were to consider this gift of choosing to choose as a challenge to make informed choices? Perhaps the whole idea of choosing is predicated on this responsibility and accountability, as well as in consideration of potential consequences of those choices. This is an intentional and multi-stepped process involving our initiative and thoughtfulness, not just a gift to be opened and used at will. If this is so, then clearly "free" choice includes limits, boundaries and structure. In consideration of all of these factors, we freely choose to make intentional and informed choices with our capacity of free choice.

This balance and more refined, some may say limited understanding of free choice can even be found within the rhythm of our Jewish year and its celebrations. Think for a moment of the annual pattern of the Jewish calendar between the holiday of **Pesach**/Passover and that of **Shavuot** as well as the seven weeks that divide them. One of the names for **Pesach** is **Zeman Cheiruteinu** or Time of our Freedom. This celebrates and observes the most pivotal historical experience in which Jewish slaves escaped from their Egyptian masters, following a new path in much the same way that Abraham did, forging a new future for themselves and their children. While they, through their own initiative, actions, and choice, and with the guidance and direction of God, were released from the oppressive hand of the Egyptians, this freedom that was so hard won was primarily a physical freedom. Freedom to worship as they pleased, to follow God, and to grow and continue as a Jewish nation were inextricably linked and rooted in this physical freedom, but would have to be actualized through intentional actions and initiatives.

Additionally, these later freedoms also entailed discipline, that is, the adherence to the laws and dictates of this God that they were now free to worship. This story of **Pesach** and the escape of the Jewish people from Egyptian slavery is not complete without the complementary story of Shavuot and its celebration of the acceptance of the Jewish nation of the rule and the laws of God as explained generally in the ***Aseret HaDibrot*** /Ten Commandments and more specifically in the six hundred and thirteen laws that define Judaism. **Shavuot** is also called ***Zeman Matan Torateinu***, the time of the giving of our Torah. This celebration of the acceptance of the laws and dictates of God is what completes and gives purpose to the story of **Pesach** and its important and timeless lesson about the freedom of the enslaved Jewish nation. While thinking of this evolving of a nation, we must remember the warnings from earlier in this chapter of those who will too often to choose to allow their capacity for choice limited to such an extreme that they no longer have such agency. This is an attraction for many to be sure, thus the success of so many Fundamentalist groupings in our world.

If the Jewish nation were to leave Egypt just to freely wander about aimlessly and without accountability or a mission to fulfill, the story would have most likely ended there and the people at the center of this powerful drama would have probably disappeared. However, the fact that they needed the physical freedom to make informed choices in terms of their spiritual and religious future – this is the most poignant aspect of this season and the sequencing of these observances. It is the appreciation and use of these freedoms that insured that there would be more of a story to tell and more generations to insure the continuity of the Jewish story and people, as is the case with other aspects of the larger Jewish story as cited in these essays. A similar case could clearly be made if we consider how the story of Avraham continues, with him not leaving his past for a completely uncertain future without boundaries; but rather to follow God, that is using his capacity of free choice to make an informed decision.

So, what exactly is informed choice and what part is played by our freedom to choose it? Choice itself entails responsibility as well as understanding that every choice will bring with it an inherent set of consequences and results. Freedom to choose should not be confused with freedom from these consequences and results of our choices that are freely made. Our freedom to choose wisely or poorly is what we need to consider with reason and calm. The fact that we live in a culture, time and nation in which freedom to choose and its opportunity is valued and considered a natural benefit of our humanity is not to be dismissed nor taken lightly. Further, it is hoped and intended that the exercise of responsibility in using this freedom of choice is what will lead us to make well informed and appropriate choices while enabling us to continue to be productive and live fulfilling lives. The balance of the individual and the community in which the individual lives as productive and constructive will be dependent on the interfacing of this process of informed choosing in a purposeful and deliberate manner on the part of all members of that community.

Questions for Continued Thought and Discussion:

1. What is your understanding of the nature of God's regrets?

2. Can you articulate the difference between free choice and informed choosing?

3. Which do you think is truly the intent of **Bechirah Chofshit** (our given capacity to choose) and the place of both the good inclination and not-so-good or not-so-satisfied inclination (*yetzer tov* and *yetzer hara*) in this in the human equation?

4. How do you balance the freedom of choice and an understanding of its consequences and outcomes in your life?

5. How do you teach and show others to do the same?

IV. Rules and Regulations

Surely this instruction, which I give to you this day, is not too difficult for you, nor is it beyond your reach.
It is not in the heavens that you should say "Who among us can go up to the heavens and get it for us and teach it to us, that we may observe it?
Neither is it beyond the sea, that you should say "Who among us can cross to the other side of the sea and get it for us and impart it to us, that we may observe it?"
No the thing is very close to you

Deuteronomy 30: 11 - 14

Rules and regulations, all part of this instruction, are central to Jewish living. This system is meant to enhance and protect life, not compromise or detract from it. While these laws are given by God through the vehicle of his designated Lawgiver Moshe, the hope, especially at the end of the Torah's narrative is that we as individuals will be so imbued with the basic understanding and investment in the foundations of these rules and regulations that they will indeed feel "very close" to us.

Many would and do posit that the presence of rules and regulations further limit our **free** or **informed choice** or render it useless altogether. Others simply do not like to have the parameters of their life and potential structured by boundaries and standards; living at the other end of the continuum of choice from those that choose to hand over their agency of choice to others. So, we must ask why do we have these restrictions on our lives? Do we even need them or can't we, as thinking and aware human beings, be left to our own devices to decide what is right and wrong, and how we should act?

Why or why not? Okay, this is not really all that difficult. Let's remember what we have already discussed regarding what free or informed choice is and is not. As we have just learned, choosing responsibly and in an informed manner is the best and most constructive way we can use this gift of choice, serving positive purposes both for the individual and the groups to which the individual belongs. Cultural anthropologists make the point again and again that it is precisely the system of rules and regulations that insure the continuity of a given people and their culture. While systems of organization will differ and people will live in castes, tribes, incorporated states, structured monarchies, covenantal states or other entities, there will be conditions set for continued life in those structures in the form of rules and regulations.

Given the experience of our contemporary world and the legacy of our history, one could easily make the point that if every person were truly to choose freely without limits and without any reservation regarding consequences, we could and most likely would all potentially be in grave danger. In fact as we have discussed, we have repeatedly witnessed exactly this dynamic in our world. What if one's free choice to plant a garden wherever one freely chooses to do so usurps another's ownership of a plot of land? What if one freely chooses to break into a store to take clothes one freely wants and for which one freely chooses not to pay? What if one freely chooses to take on the persona and position of a professional medical doctor while freely choosing not to train properly for such a position and then being looked to and depended upon by others for help and relief from serious illness? We know all too well that these things do indeed happen daily and further, we get the point. There are more serious and potentially negative ramifications for us all, if free choice is truly unfettered and well ... completely free of consequences, understanding of impact of our actions on others, and all ramifications of our own interest inspired initiatives on our larger community.

To witness this daily, all we have to do is open and read the daily newspaper, filled with reports of people who freely make such choices to kill, steal, embezzle, commit fraud and so on, continually assaulting our general society and collective sense of well-being. So, what is the nature of that *free choice* which allows all of us to simultaneously choose freely and live safely and constructively? How do we negotiate and balance the freedom of choice that allows one to define and strive for those things that one wants while the consequences of such choices are not invasive or limiting to another member of our human family who is and should be exercising the very same rights and options? What about places and spaces where people, human beings just like us, do not have any such right of choosing freely and realizing their dreams because others freely choose to make their situation as it is? Further, what responsibility, according to Jewish thinking and dictates, do we have towards the people who do not enjoy the benefit of these important and necessary human rights?

If one believes and accepts that God ordained that humans should choose freely, it is virtually impossible to justify those human beings who ordain that such rights should be removed, especially when they would affirm that they are doing so in the name of God. Is that not the ultimate insult of trying to "play God?" Look at our society today and what happens when such is done in the name of religious righteousness, as is the case in too many Fundamentalist Religious regimes and groupings. In these situations, we must look at who takes the authority to ordain how others will live and what right such people do or do not have to take on this role. What motivates them, remembering earlier discussions about desire and tangible rewards that one might be seeking by such actions, will often be factors such as control and assuredness of one's power. It is interesting to note that in Hebrew, the word/root for permission and authority is the same (*r – sh- t*). In a democracy, with all of its shortcomings, authority comes from permission. In dictatorial regimes, only authority gives or does not grant permission. To be sure, there is a thin line between how one uses and balances both of these elements.

An internalized sense of responsibility and accountability is clearly what would help us discern this thin line. That sense of responsibility and accountability has to incorporate every aspect of our world – including the other beings who live in it and with whom we share space, our environment, the elements of our universe on which we are dependent and of course, in terms of our understanding of what God Who Created Us wants from us. In line with the expectations of the cultural anthropologists, clearly Judaism has its system of rules and regulations to help us maintain this balance. That being said, Maimonides teaches that it is impossible to structure every single action in which we engage as a rule or regulation. Those who follow the very complex and intricate system of Jewish Law know this well; there will always be new situations in which we will need to understand the "correct way" to act. Here is where reason comes to our rescue and we use that shared understanding with God who created us to act in an appropriate manner. Rabbi Sir Jonathan Sacks teaches that here there is a true test of what we are, namely how we act at all times. He states as follows:

> There is a danger in a religion like Judaism, with so many clear-cut rules for highly specific situations, that we may forget that there are areas of life which have no rules, only role-models, but which are no less religiously significant for that One of the great Jewish mystics, Rabbi Leib Saras, used to say that he travelled to Rabbi Dov Baer of Mezeritch, not to learn Biblical interpretations but to see how the Rabbi tied his shoelaces. (21)

Obviously, we have to consider and come to recognize that limits and boundaries are needed to keep all uses of free choice in check as we acknowledge that we live in a world with many different peoples and ideas of what is the correct way to live. Further, even the most complete set of rules and regulations will not be a panacea for anything that might go awry. With the best of intentions or the most banal of motivations, we are further reminded that many of those ideas as well as programs of rules and regulations that may evolve from them are framed within the context of one's perception of his or her ultimate responsibility to God or whatever Higher Power one submits to or believes in, That Creator of all that we are and have.

Consider the following statement that you have probably heard before: "God understands and accepts me; it's the neighbors I am not quite sure about." Let's really think about this sentiment for a moment. Within our various religious groupings there are many different perspectives regarding how and when one may choose and one may not, what actions are acceptable and how one should perform such prescribed actions. Throughout our history we have well documented records of such groupings fighting for their sole position as the rightful proprietors of what is correct and acceptable within their religious framework. Each religious grouping has a history replete with examples of such conflicts, including noble defense of The Creator as well as implementation of personal agendas that cannot be ignored or obliterated in terms of their effects from the pages of our history.

Throughout time, a sort of understood hierarchy has emerged in many of our religious communities regarding who represents the most correct understanding of the desire of The One to whom a group claims allegiance. However, one must be careful in terms of yielding to such claims and the ones who make them. Even within the most religious and structured sectors of such groupings, we do not find unanimity regarding the content and intent of the word of God, so this must tell us something significant. Rather, we must note that too often, we find vigorous debate regarding this dynamic.

In a rather familiar text to many, we learn in the words of the Talmud as follows:

> For three years Beit Hillel and Beit Shammai debated each other. The first party said 'The law follows our view.' The second party said, 'The law follows our view.' A heavenly voice came out and said, 'These and those are the words of the Living God, and the law is according to Beit Hillel." But if these and those are the words of the Living God, because of what reason did Beit Hillel merit the fixing of the law according to their view? This merit was granted them because they were comforting and modest, and they would study their own rulings and the rulings of Beit Shammai. Not only that, but they would mention the opinions of Beit Shammai before their own.
>
> Tractate Eruvim, 13b, Babylonian Talmud

Notice the reasons that the words and rulings and the resulting stated perception of truth of Beit Hillel (the students of Hillel) were the benchmark for Jewish law. Beit Hillel considered all of the various possibilities and perspectives, even giving credence and precedence to as well as incorporating those different points of view that might have conflicted with their perception of truth. This process of consideration and incorporation of the other's point of view and reconciling it with one's own is oft repeated throughout the Talmud on the part of many of the important teachers' whose legacies are found there. What an important lessons for us to consider in our own lives, that different people may have various perspectives to contribute to the collective process of determining how we can best live as well as develop our perception of truth, while translating that truth into the rules and regulations that guide and structure our lives.

Further, clearly there is a sense and understanding of the presence and importance of rules and regulations here, as the various positions of Beit Hillel and Beit Shammai cited are in relation to how one interprets and develops Jewish law from its original source, the Torah. In fact the discussion in which this quoted text and teaching is found is about boundaries and how they are implemented in Jewish life as standards for daily living. In Jewish living and learning, the Talmud is all about rules and regulations and how we develop the practices and observances that will help us incorporate these Torah given standards in our lives and set appropriate boundaries in an ongoing manner. The rules and regulations are to lead us to living a life well, which can only be done with the proper motivation as a human being who is even concerned with a detail as seemingly insignificant as how he or she ties his shoes.

Further, within these codes are found different and even opposing interpretations, though there is agreement regarding the source of accountability, namely the word of God. We know well that other groups and faith communities have analogous codes of living. The degree to which these codes include discussion and even debate about these standards varies significantly within different religious systems, and the obvious value and prominence of such in the Talmud is one of the most powerful benchmarks of **Halacha**/Jewish law and how it is developed, recognized as such by the Jewish faith community and others as well; including for example, a Muslim writer by the name of Irshad Manji, as we discussed earlier.

For the Native Americans, there is a different way of looking at this basic element of our lives. For them, such regulatory standards are seen as being ingrained naturally in their behaviors and interaction with each other and the land on which they live. In fact, their teachers have indicated that, according to their observations of the "white man," they basically discern such stated and written codes of rules and regulations to be externally mandated maxims that have little to do with actual behaviors and initiatives that are nurturing and supportive of the members of the group that abides (or does not do so) by such standards and expectations.

One writing in which this perspective is expressed follows:

> Oral-based knowledge systems are predominant among First Nations. Stories are frequently told as evening family entertainment to pass along local or family knowledge. Stories are also told more formally, in ceremonies such as potlatches, to validate a person's or family's authority, responsibilities, or prestige.
>
> Some stories are told only during certain seasons, at a particular time of day, or in specific places. In the same vein, some stories are to be heard only by specific people. Such stories often teach important lessons about a given society's culture, the land, and the ways in which members are expected to interact with each other and their environment. The passing on of these stories from generation to generation keeps the social order intact. As such, oral histories must be told carefully and accurately; often by a designated person who is recognized as holding this knowledge. This person is responsible for keeping the knowledge and eventually passing it on in order to preserve the historical record. (22)

For them, the "rules and regulations" of their lives are the learned and accepted behaviors that are passed down from generation to generation as continued traditions and practices from their role models. Their elders have questioned what possible power could a written document have that is more potent than the authority of personally transmitted generational teachings. Perhaps they understand the adage that "any contract is only as good and honorable as the people who have affixed their signatures to it." For them, generational teachings are precisely this contract, more honorable than many, if not all, written codes by virtue of its constant presence and vitality in the life of their community as well as in the relationships that build and identify that community in an ongoing way from generation to generation.

By the way, it is important to note that this ongoing transmission from generation to generation (***midor ledor***) is the foundational basis of Jewish teaching of rules and regulations. As a point of clarification, many would claim that the written record just documents it. In fact, the "Oral Torah" or Talmud is a record that actually narrates the power and authority of this generational transmission of knowledge and standards of behavior to be observed by all, based on the collective experience of the Jewish nation dating back to their very earliest beginnings. Until fairly recently even within many segments of the Orthodox communal continuum, the holders of traditions and teachings were the familial authorities, the mothers and the fathers of their respective families. As the Jewish communal generational breakdown occurred, family and community entities became more mobile, and rules and regulations were relaxed. In response to this void, as seen in analogous cases cited by Robert Bly from the context of our American society, direct Rabbinic authority has become more central and present in our communities today. The purpose of this influence, when exercised correctly, is optimally to insure the continuation of our collective legacy and its many components as well as the rules and regulations that emanate from it. But we would be remiss if we did not note that this too can and unfortunately sometimes does devolve into lack of responsible use of limited power and agency, subject to the God given law that directs this process.

In looking at our own contemporary reality as citizens in a Western democracy, we learn from the earliest age about the importance of rules and regulations in our lives, while balancing them with the making of informed choices. We learn that as we become part of community and take our place as a contributing member of that community, rules and regulations will help to insure that we can live together as a collective. Our teachers are our parents, teachers, older siblings, and others who model the behaviors that we will follow, while developing a sense of right and wrong. This is the generational teaching that insures the continuation of the written contract or code of rules and regulations, and that to which Rabbi Sacks refers.

As an example, let's think about the development and scripting of our primary and elementary school experiences for just a moment. As we move from pre-school through Kindergarten and the early years of our educational experience through third grade, there is much emphasis on the development of self, choosing appropriately and responsibly, and being a cooperative member of a larger group. In so doing, we learn about the need to observe the rules and regulations that help us discipline ourselves in a manner so that we can balance the freedom of self so valued in our Western democratic society with the safety and viability of the group to which we belong. As students move from their focus on *me* to understanding that they are a part of a much larger *we*, there is a growing sense of responsibility as well as empowerment, with a strong sense of the need to interface the two elements of self and group continually and consistently.

Once again, this is a matter of balance. Namely by being a good and constructive group member, I will be more of a "player" in the larger group. The following of that group's rules and regulations simultaneously may and will "limit" my personal freedom, but also enhances my personal sense of self by group validation. This is why we teach children from the earliest age that "two heads are better than one" or how much more the group can accomplish by working together versus individual and separate efforts. By the way, this value is strongly expressed within Jewish texts and lore.

In **Kohelet**/Ecclesiastes, we read as follows in chapter 4, verses 9 – 12:

> Two are better than one, for they have a good reward for their labor. For if they fall, the one will lift up his friend; and woe to the one who falls and there is no one to pick him up. Also, if two lie together there is heat for them; and if one is alone, there is no warmth. If (another) one challenges, two shall withstand him; and a threefold cord will not be easily broken.

The lesson is clear here in terms of the power and the strength of the group as a collection of invested individuals. Further, throughout Jewish tradition and texts, we see many examples of how the group and its adherence to established rules and regulations enhances the individual, while Judaism itself is so defined by the group that maintains its dictates. This can work either in favor of the group or to its detriment. Consider the well-known incident of the Golden Calf in which the group does not act on behalf of its own good.

In **Shemot**/ Exodus 32: 1 – 4, we read about this most painful chapter in Jewish history as follows:

> The people saw that Moses was not coming down from the mountain, and the nation gathered against Aaron and they said to him, "Go and make for us a god who shall go before us, because that man Moses brought us from the land of Egypt, and we do not know what happened to him. And Aaron said to them, Take off the gold rings that are in the ears of your wives, your sons and your daughters, and bring them to me. All the people [did so] ... and cast [the gold] into a mold and make it into a calf. And they explained,

> "This is your god, Israel, that brought you from the land of Egypt."

Clearly this group did not act in accordance with the regulations that were to define the essence of their being. Notice that God is not even mentioned here; it is Moses and his absence that the people are responding to in their reactions. So the very chain of command, which begins with God is clearly broken and the people are acting of their own accord and within the context of their own panic. Further, their actions resemble those of the other peoples around them, not being at all reflective of the parameters determined to govern their own group identity. Aaron's actions are seriously questioned, the people are punished and there would be repercussions for such ill-founded initiative in this situation and in many others to come throughout our history.

It is interesting to parenthetically note that immediately after this event, we read volumes about the extremely careful detail and instructions regarding the building of the Mishkan, the tabernacle that would join the group together and define them as a collective entity in many ways. Apparently, more instruction, that is additional rules and regulations were needed for the well-being of the group, as the body of instructions that they had at their disposal at this point were not enough to guide them through every possible situation. That being said, this problem will definitely repeatedly appear as the text of the Tanach continues. Further, it is one that still plays out in our lives throughout history until today.

As one of many examples that could be chosen as this Biblical narrative continues, consider that later in Joshua, we see that the group does not take the initiative to influence and ultimately stop a group member by the name of Achan who is about to act against the rules clearly laid out in the Torah by taking spoils of war, definitely against the prescribed dictates of the Jewish nation in situations of conflict and war.

In Joshua, Chapter 7, we read as follows:

> And the LORD said unto Joshua: 'Get up; now, why have you fallen upon your face? **11** Israel has sinned; they have transgressed My covenant, which I commanded them; they have taken of the forbidden spoils of war; and have also stolen, and even put it among their own stuff. **12** Therefore … I will not be with you any more, except if you destroy the accursed from among you. **13** Up, sanctify the people, and say: Sanctify yourselves against tomorrow; for thus says the LORD, the God of Israel: There is a curse in the midst of you, O Israel; you cannot stand before your enemies, until you take away the accursed thing from among you. **…15** It shall be that he that is with the forbidden booty shall be burnt with fire, he and all that he has; because he has transgressed the covenant of the LORD, and because he has wrought harm in Israel.' **16** So Joshua rose up early in the morning, and brought Israel near by their tribes; and the tribe of Judah was taken. **…** and Achan, the son of Carmi, the son of Zabdi, the son of Zerah, of the tribe of Judah, was taken. **19** And Joshua said unto Achan: 'My son, give, I pray thee, glory to the LORD, the God of Israel, and make confession unto God; and tell me now what thou hast done; hide nothing from me.' **20** And Achan answered Joshua, and said: 'Of a truth I have sinned against the LORD, the God of Israel, and this is what I have done. **21** When I saw among the spoil good … [things], then I coveted them, and took them; and, behold, they are hid in the earth in the midst of my tent,...' **22** Joshua sent messengers, and they ran unto the tent; and, behold, it was hid in his tent ....' And all Israel stoned him with stones…
> [Translation is adapted from JPS]

So what went so terribly wrong for poor Achan? The entire community is held accountable for not stopping him from crossing the set boundaries and taking the spoils of war, which was clearly against the set rules and regulations. In the Gemara, in Shabbat 53b – 54b we learn that the greatest leaders of the Jewish nation were held responsible for passing up the opportunity to hold others back if and when they crossed unacceptable boundaries. The rules and regulations were for all to uphold and protect for the collective good as well as for the good of the members of the collective. As a result of this lack of group or individual initiative and taking of responsibility, Achan perishes and the entire Jewish people will suffer at the next battle against Ai, which they should have easily won.

We learn here and in so many other instances that there is a responsibility of the group towards the individual built into the system of Jewish life that simply cannot be ignored. There are many other such examples that reflect this similar dynamic throughout the Jewish narrative, as there are instances when the influence of the group does work in favor of the individuals who are part of the collective whole. This was the goal of the leaders, the prophets and all those who tried to communicate the will of God to this people who were invested with the task of discerning and acting according to that will. This is the basis of Ethical Monotheism that so defines the Jewish perception of God as imminent and part of our lives, brought into our world through the actions and initiatives that we take according to God's wishes and goals for us and consistent with the rules and regulations that are ordained for the good of individuals as well as the collective whole.

Further, in a somewhat different venue, those of us who remember particularly difficult moments in our history as a group of Americans can testify to the fact that even when a President is assassinated, or a

President must resign, or an election cannot be immediately decided for a variety of reasons, life still goes on virtually uninterrupted and we all continue to live by the written code of rules and regulations that govern our group, in this case, the citizenry of the United States of America. True, these rules and regulations are written on paper, as is characteristic of constitutional democracy. However, they "work" due to the honor and understanding and accepted teachings of the citizenry that lives by them, similar to the case of generational transmission discussed above. Were it not for that honor and understanding as exemplified by the members, the role models if you will, in our society, this set of rules and regulations would not be able to successfully govern the citizenry.

There are most important lessons to be learned here as well as clear contrasts to other governments, systems, and countries in which such moments of tension and vulnerability produce chaos and uncertainty, not an opportunity to test the order and success of the dictates by which a given group lives. These moments bring a sense of pride in what we are collectively, as well as testimony to the value of the rules and regulations by which we live. As we have seen, this can be true when transmission is based on group will and adherence to God's commanded actions as is the case with the Jewish nation; when generational transmission is strictly oral and based upon the authority of elders in the community of Native Americans; or in the case of a constitutional democracy such as the United States of America. Rabbi Lord Jonathan Sacks speaks about this phenomenon as that of covenantal community, where all members of the community are tied by a shared covenant to which all are accountable and for which all are responsible to maintain. In the absence of these elements, a group, a nation or a collective of individuals can and indeed have succumbed to the throes of chaos as well as possibly abdicated all rights to the power of the entity that would usurp all power for itself.

Moving back to the more mundane elements of our daily lives, consider the most interesting phenomenon of traffic lights for a moment. Here is a wonderful and oft-used example of how rules and regulations are operative in our lives, at times on the "honor system" model. Obviously, we all understand the purpose of traffic lights, especially when there is a significant flow of traffic. Most of the time, people honor this "regulation" of our lives and when this is not the case, there can be and at times are dire consequences. However, we are all familiar with the question regarding if you are driving on a seemingly deserted road without any traffic at an obviously off-peak hour, and the traffic light "instructs" you to stop and there are no police in sight, what do you do? Of course, there can always be another motorist who "appears out of nowhere" but nonetheless and aside from this possibility, this is actually an interesting question to consider with people regarding how we perceive and honor our own expected standards of behavior. Are the same rules and regulations always equally needed? Perhaps not, but it is important to have consistency in terms of expectations and understanding of how we need to function so that our choices and group safety are both accommodated as much as possible. Learned habitual behaviors, such as stopping appropriately at traffic lights or abiding by constitutional mandates for hard to resolve elections or sharing our resources because our Jewish system of law tells us to do so all contribute to the achievement of this balance in our group existence; consistently and simultaneously protecting the rights of individuals and group.

Rules and regulations indeed serve many critically needed purposes. This is clearly acknowledged in Jewish Law. It is a known phenomenon that the rules and regulations of Jewish living address virtually every aspect of our lives. How one eats, uses time, dresses, relates to their spouse, speaks to others through the course of the day, observes days of celebration, and so many other matters are all accommodated and explained in great detail in extensive codes, literature, Rabbinic position papers, and so forth. These standards, rules and regulations are learned by observation and generation transmission of the actual behaviors. Further, as stated earlier, this generational transmission and inherent role modeling of proper behaviors will maintain both the spirit as well as the letter of the law, so that when a situation arises that is not "covered," and it will in fact happen, we will know what to do as we extend the reach of established and known rules and practices into new territory.

This is the elasticity and expansion of the reach of the codes and defined practices within Jewish Law that Irshad Manji finds lacking in Islam. By contrast, as Yeshayahu Leibowitz echoes what so many others teach us, Judaism and its system of law, Halacha, is dedicated to doing just this:

> The first mark of the religion of Halacha is its realism. It perceives man as he is in reality and confronts him with this reality – with the actual conditions of his existence rather than the 'vision' of another existence. Religion is concerned with the status, the function, and the duties of man, as constrained by these circumstances. It precludes the possibility of man's shirking his duties by entertaining illusions of attaining a higher level of being. The religion of Halacha is concerned with man and addresses him in his drab day-by-day existence... The Mitzvot require observance out of a sense of duty and discipline, not ecstatic enthusiasm or fervor... (23)

While many find this pervasive code of living to be meaningful and observe so much of what is written and handed to us through our generations as developed laws and practices, it is no secret that others perceive this as limiting personal freedoms and even group existence excessively. This range of perception has greatly polarized the larger Jewish community in our contemporary society as well as during other times in our history and created rifts between groups of Jews that can often be quite painful and sometimes perceived to be irreconcilable. What one group or some individuals may see as the accepted rules and regulations that allow them to live a more meaningful and purposeful life given the reality of who we are and our limits, such a system may and will appear to be exclusive and insulting to another. Often enough, colleagues have remarked to me that in primarily Jewish settings such as day schools or synagogues, there are groups of individuals who seem to take on a type of ***protectsia*** and exclude those who "do not meet their standards." This is NOT the intended outcome of this system of law and praxis. Quite the contrary, we are continually taught that our laws and dictates are to keep us humble and remind us of our need to be concerned for and care for and include each other. Remember what Rabbi Leib Saras wanted to learn from Rabbi Dov Baer of Mezeritch – not intellectual readings of a text or complex matters of Jewish law, but just how he went through a day and acted at every juncture, including how he performed the simple task of putting on his shoes.

Consider the many situations that occur in which people from these different groups come together. In the workplace, those that observe Jewish rules and regulations (what we have identified as the ***Halacha***) more stringently may not be able to join their co-workers for lunch at the restaurant in town or go to a Friday night office social. Often within circles of friends and certainly families, different levels of observance and correlative adherence to the various rules and regulations of the pervasive and detailed system of Jewish Law will challenge the planning of a special event at which some may need special accommodations (to observe dietary laws) or may not be able to attend (if doing so would compromise one's observance of the details of **Shabbat** or **Yom Tov** or occur during a time of limited social involvement such as **Sefirat HaOmer** or the ***Nine Days***). Even something as basic as Jewish identity and the conditions of that identity can and do divide our community for understood reasons but nonetheless with pain and conflict.

Many families talk about the challenge, and for many the pain, of what happens when those who are more observant of the rules and regulations of **Halacha** interface with those whose lives are not so directly dictated by these rules and regulations or those who maintain different interpretations of this multi-tiered system of living. Clearly, one has to address some very real issues here regarding one's choices, priorities, and one's sense of discipline and adherence to these rules and regulations. It is extremely difficult, for example, for many who drive and participate in the secular world on Shabbat and Jewish holidays to understand, even accept those who do not, and vice versa. Often there is a feeling of being slighted personally when the actual issue is that there are different levels of acceptance and understanding and "buy in" regarding these rules and regulations that have been defined as being the content of Jewish observance.

To be sure, there is responsibility involved on all sides regarding how the various parties in such potential conflicts "freely choose" to come to terms with the situation and in their understanding of the rules and regulations that govern their lives. For those who are more observant of the rules and regulations of Jewish Law, it is supremely important to remember that there are both those commanded actions of **Mitzvot** that involve how we interact with God, called **Mitzvot Bein Adam LaMakom**, as well as those that dictate how we interact with our fellow Jews and members of the larger human family, referred to in Jewish Law/Halacha as **Mitzvot Bein Adam LeChavero**. Often the kindness and consideration we use in explaining and living through some of these differences will determine how those explanations are accepted and understood by our friends and families.

Unfortunately, one of the characteristics of Religious Fundamentalism within many of our religious communities is that one might become so zealous about observance of the commandments between man and God (***Mitzvot Bein Adam LaMakom***) that the commandments between man and man (***Mitzvot Bein Adam LeChavero***) might not be emphasized nor practiced to the degree that they should be, interestingly enough though they are accorded the same degree of importance as the former category of rules and regulations. Included in the same code of rules and regulations about eating, dress, observance of holidays and so much else, are also just as complete and complex codes regarding how we should speak to each other, how we are obligated to behave in our business dealings, how we are to act honorably towards one another, our responsibility to help and ease the pain of others and so forth. In fact there are many cases where our responsibilities towards each other will take precedence over the purely ritualistic aspects of our lives.

As a primary example, consider that one extremely clear standard of behavior is that we are not to embarrass each other or any human being with whom we have contact, for God is at the core of every being and therefore when we insult one of God's created beings, we offend God. Imagine if every Jew who is religiously observant in a ritual sense and observes all of the standards of Halacha would be as attentive to this Halacha as some of the others previously indicated. Remembering that the intent of this system is that all commanded actions are of significant and compelling value as well as interrelated to and interdependent on one another, one would be hard pressed to not attach such value to this standard and the ***mitzvot*** that emanate from it. Think for a moment of how adherence to this one standard would help to structure the manner regarding how one would deal with some of the various conflicts indicated in the larger discussion represented here.

Let us consider the *mitzvah* of "and you will love your neighbor as yourself" as stated in *VaYikra* 19:18. Look for a moment at the larger context of this well-known dictum. It appears in **Parshat Kedoshim** in which we are reminded to act in a sanctified and proper way in all manner of our daily dealings because God acts that way and in so doing we are fulfilling what God wants of us. The entire verse from which this well-known teaching comes as well as the ones preceding and following reads as follows:

> You shall not hate your brother in your heart. Admonish your colleague about their wrongdoing but do not incur wrongdoing in doing so. You will not take vengeance or bear a grudge against any of your countrymen and ***you will love your neighbor as yourself,*** I am the Lord. You shall observe my laws. (Leviticus 19: 17 – 19a)

So, how easy is it to follow these dictates, not just say the words, as nice as they may sound? What does this mean in terms of our actions? I often make the statement (and remember that this idea is set forth by an observant Jew by any measure) that when considering, for example, the extensive dietary laws/***Kashrut*** that determine what a ritualistically observant Jew eats, "we should worry at least half as much about what comes out of our mouth as what goes in it." This is a direct reference to the equally extensive (and far more difficult to follow) set of rules and regulations governing our speech, or ***Shmirat HaLashon***, which include among many components the injunction of not embarrassing another human being for we are all made ***BeTzelem Elokim***, that is in the image of God. By embarrassing another, not only are we breaking a commandment between fellow human beings but also between us and God, The Creator of the being we are potentially hurting through our speech.

Imagine if there was a requirement for the correlative observance of the rules that govern the relationship between man and God and those that define the relationship between human beings. Just consider the collective impact if every member of the Jewish community who was learning about and incorporating the entire code of behaviors and standards of **Halacha** in their lives would be held accountable by such an equation. Well guess what! There is just such a requirement that all of these commanded actions are equally important. Not only that, but in effect all *mitzvot* are about man's relationship to God, so in a very real sense, when one ignores, breaks or does not otherwise observe a *Mitzvah Bein Adam LeChavero,* that person is also slighting a *Mitzvah Bein Adam LaMakom*!

As people within the Jewish community become increasingly observant, too often (though certainly not always but this should not be the case at all!) there is tremendous focus on the ritually focused commandments that are between man and God such as the strictest possible observance of Shabbat, Kashrut, modest dress, and so forth. Let us all respectively campaign for equal attention to the rules and regulations regarding honesty and proper action in our business transactions, respectful and loving interactions with family and deeds of kindness and sharing and caring for others. Further, let's invite our friends and neighbors of other faith communities to follow our example and join this worthy campaign!

As an illustration of what has gone terribly wrong in our truly wonderful system of rules and regulations, several authorities and colleagues within the religiously observant Jewish community have begun to be disturbed by the increased prison population of observant Jews. Now, granted, this population remains quite small, even tiny, in comparison to other groupings. However, with a growth of religious prayer communities or full *Minyanim* available in our prison system, one has to wonder how those who live by such an all-inclusive system of rules and regulations can land in such a community. When one chaplain inquired about this phenomenon, one prisoner simply and boldly stated, "Well, embezzlement is not prohibited by Jewish Law." Of course, this is not in any way true! However, in reading the words of Torah extremely narrowly and being overly concerned with our relationship to God, it is indeed possible for one to fall into the trap of being so misguided as to think that this is so.

Consider how a young student took the law into his own hands more than twenty years ago and murdered Yitzchak Rabin (may his memory be for a blessing) by stating that he had Rabbinic permission to kill him because his actions were immediately threatening Jewish lives. After this horrific set of events, many Rabbis and leaders in the Orthodox Jewish community as well as other parts of the larger Jewish community expressed their concern about how language is used and the need to be careful and vigilant regarding how one is able to influence others through their own diatribes and verbal attacks. In other words, there was an active campaign for the observance of the laws of **Shemirat HaLashon** (how we speak) in the Jewish community, too often forgotten and not used. There are, sadly enough, too many other examples of similar reasoning and terrible results as an outcome of not being mindful of such potential effects of what is said. Unfortunately the change in focus in the community as a result of taking account of ourselves, taking a **Heshbon HaNefesh**, is too often way too short lived.

Clearly this is yet another "abuse" in taking personal prerogatives in definitively deciding what one has the authority to do or not do within the frame of the system of rules and regulations to which one is supposedly accountable. What right, we must ask, does one have to say, "I know the truth" or "I know what the law says and will take it into my own hands!" Part of the very inclusive and extensive system of Halacha has everything to do with authority and the need to listen to and follow the ways of the teachers and previous generations and NOT to make such decisions for one self, engaging in a personally ordained from of vigilantism. In fact, embedded in so many Talmudic discussions is the attempt to figure out exactly what we are and what we are ***not*** to do according to the words and authority of our texts and their teaching, focusing on the discipline of the word more than the potential power of the individual and its possible misuse. Looking outside of this clearly defined system, once again, we see many such examples of individuals taking such license in exercising their "individual freedom" in "acting upon" the rules and regulations by which they claim to be governed.

When looking at our established codes of rules and regulations and acknowledging the element of choice in our lives in following them, it is also imperative that we are clear about what we are not enabled to decide for ourselves. To be sure, there are choices to be made while we are also to acknowledge the discipline of the system to which we claim allegiance. Otherwise, the very balance that such codes of rule and regulations are intended to achieve will be compromised severely to the point of rendering the codes themselves ineffectual. We need to see and understand the powerful element of discipline in how we use our ability to choose, as must others with whom we interact. This is the place of rules and regulations in our lives.

Questions for Continued Thought and Discussion:

1. What do you understand to be the connection between informed choice as discussed previously and the place of rules and regulations as explored in this chapter?

2. Can you make a case for such a system of rules and regulations enabling society and individuals to be the best they can be? Can you make a case where such a system would not engender such a goal?

3. What do you think Rabbi Lord Jonathan Sacks means when he talks about a "covenantal community?"

4. How can rules and regulations that are in place and govern the group or collective actually help us to live more freely?

V. When My Childhood Is Your History

A generation goes and a generation comes,
And the earth stands forever…
Whatever has been will be and what has been done will be done
And there is nothing new under the sun.

Kohelet/Ecclesiastes, Chapter 1, verses 4, 9

I often explain that one of the most important reasons that I have chosen to work in the field of education, as my lifelong professional endeavor, is that I am the archetypal eternal student. Therefore, I used to love to sit in the library throughout the school day during the many years when I was teaching in schools, or to be more precise, facilitating the process of learning together with others, and learn at will. Surrounded by books and the thoughts and wisdom of others I do my best work in thinking, learning, writing and preparing for the next chapter of life and wherever it may take me. One day some time ago, I am sitting, immersed in my work while one of my colleagues advises, cajoles and guides her students as they learn about a long ago age known as the "sixties" in which, of course, they feel no personal investment and of which they have no direct knowledge. At the end of her session with her students, I approached her and asked how she feels when "our childhood is history for her students." She laughed and that was the end of our conversation but certainly not the end of my thinking about this question, which may have sounded pithy but clearly was not so.

We know very well that cycles continue and as they say, "history repeats itself." Yes, this is a fact of our lives to a point. The problem is that we also know "to forget history is to repeat it." So, once again we are confronted with a balancing act. In our lives there is so much from our history and past experiences that we are adjured to remember and pass on, often as a context for the rules and regulations that govern our lives and the choices we make regarding them. It is this generational transmission of rules and regulations and the important lessons they teach that helps us to maintain some consistency and grounding in our lives. It is also what facilitates the process by which we, even allows us to, build and strengthen our horizontal community. It allows us to live in our present reality while building upon those lessons and experiences of the vertical community of which we are also part, namely the generations that have preceded us.

As indicated previously, one of the most potent recurrent themes in Robert Bly's book, The Sibling Society is that too often an entire generation who did not accept the ongoing teaching and instruction of their parents and teachers and other role models now acquiesce and abdicate the instructive and disciplinary roles that are theirs to exercise. This, according to Bly, is what we are seeing in too many of our current young adults who should be taking their place in the ongoing school in which we all live called life, but instead are rudderless and undirected in their own journeys, without role models and the benefit of what we have discussed as being the vital importance of generational transmission.

Bly comments as follows:

> I was surprised, as I began writing the book, that a culture run by adolescents, or by adults in an adolescent mood would treat children so badly. But in fact adolescents living in an actual family do not pay much attention to the ones "above" them, not the little ones beneath them. That is particularly true if the adolescents feel like orphans. (24)

What happens when we remove this ongoing process of generational transmission of the rules and regulations that have become honored by time, and the framework in which they operate from our new and younger members of community who are waiting and expecting to be taught how to be. This was the battle of the sixties, the phenomenon we all recall as the generation gap, some by what is written in our pages of history and others by having lived through and been part of it. The idea that somehow the older generations had nothing to say to or teach the youth of the sixties and early seventies created tension, angst and a social disconnect between these generational communities. How much was this disconnect, in retrospect, myth and how much was reality? Can one generation really walk away from those that preceded it and start anew, fully exercising their right to choose freely and without the discipline of limits, rules and lessons learned from our collective past? Does doing so bode well for such a group?

As the text from **Kohelet** at the beginning of this chapter continues, we are told that one will think that they have found something new but in fact, it is not new rather just something that was forgotten and is being rediscovered (Chapter One, verse 10). We have already discussed the importance and significance of roots to our past and the ramifications for our collective and individual health and quality of life in walking away from that past and all of its lessons. Do we really want our younger generations to grow up without memory, to have to backtrack and learn lessons that were hard learned and harder earned by those that have the wisdom yielded by going through and feeling the impact of such experiences?

Of course not! We must accept our responsibility to teach the lessons and experiences of our past generations to the younger ones. We have a tacit obligation to do so, regardless of how painful it might be. Once again, let us turn to a most difficult lesson of the larger world history arena that is necessarily part of the inheritance that we all have from our collective past. The events of the Holocaust are often well known, as are the horrors and the details of many of these horrors. What must be remembered is that aside from the use of technology in "perfecting" the efficiency of the Nazi machine, so much was not at all new, but rather repeated from earlier pages and chapters and generations of European History. The wearing of identifying badges by designated groups, exclusion from professional guilds and organizations, book burnings, forced occupancy of indicated areas called ghettos and so much else of this horrible experience are all right out of the collective history of the Middle Ages and even more recent than that.

One of the many sets of stories that are so difficult for us to hear from this more recent era of terror is that of Jewish people who recognized the signs of impending doom from past chapters of their legacies, abandoned their resources and loyalties in Europe and left, carrying with them the frustration that they often did not understand why their relatives and friends and more people who were able to do so chose instead to remain in their respective homes as opposed to listening and heeding what they considered to be the already hard learned lessons of past generations. Adding further to this painful narrative is the realization of those who knew what was happening as it began but remained quiet, the massive group of bystanders.

Hatred of entire groupings just because of who they are is a long and frightfully consistent theme in the history of mankind that is one of the more difficult aspects of our collective legacy. Clearly, we must be mindful of it and aware of its presence as well as acknowledge that we are always vulnerable to this most devastating misappropriation of human initiative.

As we revisit the first example in this chapter, that of the elements of our younger adults' generation that may not have the direction and guidance that they needed, let us return for a moment to the "sixties," which shows a different type of rejection, that of the very generational transmission we have already established as meaningful and pivotal to our healthy continuation as individuals and group members. Was this the first instance of generational rebellion against all that was associated with rules and regulations and discipline and the valuing of the past?

Of course not! A quick read of books such as Irving Howe's World of our Fathers (New York: Harcourt Brace Jovanovich, 1976) clearly indicates that this theme of rebellion existed rather pervasively in our generations of immigrants that came to the United States in the early part of the twentieth century. Howe reports about groups of kids who just "hung out," substance abuse, promiscuity and the many other behaviors associated with this "breakaway" generation of the sixties, all part of the grandparents' generation of those who lived through this more recent era.

One example of this phenomenon that he examines is the lawlessness that resulted from newfound freedoms, for which the Jewish immigrants did not have necessary skill sets. Different generations reacted as groups in widely different manners. Howe writes as follows:

> The old ones come to America "with sacred traditions; the middle-aged Jews have rigid outlooks; the youthful *istn* [political activists] have principles. But the young men without spiritual roots are defenseless against American life." (25)

This complete disassociation from the past plagued these young people who then turned to destructive behaviors, instead of utilizing the opportunity of freedom, which came to them in no small part due to the chances taken by their parents and grandparents, for achievement of greater goals. While they stood to gain so much due to the chances and risks taken by their parents and grandparents who understood the *we* for whom they were making such difficult decisions, instead the choice was often made to use the freedom gained by the hands of others to ignore everyone except *me*.

Further even a surface investigation of the Middle Ages, already briefly mentioned above, would reveal a plethora of rebellions and many attempts to break with everything that was taught and passed on as legacy to the new generations. As one example, the Peasants' Revolt of 1381 is a well-known example of a complete break as a result of frustration at a vulnerable point in history. Instead of seeing themselves as part of history, peasants in England were overcome with the frustration of the abuses they observed and to which they were subjected and would take advantage of the profound shortage of workers and devastation of the Black Death, demanding more and more money and creating profound contention, further compromising this challenging juncture of history. Though their anger and frustration were justified by many accounts, their cause became self-serving often losing the mission that may have originally motivated them. This would set their society back and not effect positive change. As Dan Jones comments in his book, Summer of Blood – The Peasants' Revolt of 1381, this is a sad story of a revolt, where even the most righteous rebels will end up thwarting their own cause. (26)

Certainly, the history of the Church and Christianity, as another much studied example, contains such chapters of disconnect embedded in its own legacy. These include the enabling of newly recognized, ill-advised and abusive leadership who broke with the past and its important lessons of understanding, humility, consideration of others, accountability to God, and so much else in its attempt to create a new society accountable to them!

Basically, the attempt to break with, and even to forget, the past goes as far back as the generations of history themselves and is documented in our earliest records of these generations. The point here is that our challenge, even mandate, is to acknowledge this attempt and respond to it in a manner that will insure and simultaneously not compromise our continuity as a people. In short, as Kohelet taught, we are hard pressed at this point, or any other through our many generations of history, to truly identify something as completely new, not rooted in the past and its history, lessons learned, experience, rules and regulations. So, simply why should we not learn from the past in order to forge into the future instead of having to continually relearn already confirmed lessons?

The perennial challenge is to consider how we keep our history, which is made up of the experiences of those who have gone before us, alive and instructive and not relegate it to a dusty top shelf in our libraries and minds. Simply, we are obligated to remember. In the Jewish community, when we talk of such destructive experiences as the Holocaust, we say "***Zachor!***" meaning "Remember!" This is good advice, to remember all of our past for its difficult lessons as well as its challenges and its instruction.

Returning for a moment to the Native American community briefly mentioned earlier, memory is critically important to them; in fact it is the means of surviving and thriving. Through their stories, passed down traditions, and collective generational experiences, memory is all about preserving the past and continuing its legacy on their shared trajectory as they move into the future. In so doing, they tie generations together both horizontally, that is across space, and vertically or across time frames. Further, it is most difficult for their elders to understand the other peoples that live around them and do not use this same method of remembering (following the instruction to "*zachor*") but rather relegate their valuable and indispensable memory to the transitory medium of paper, which they feel does often end up on the top of a dusty shelf. Living one's past continually until it becomes the present and the future IS the modus operandi of the Native American community.

As we consider the Jewish community and its legacy, throughout Torah we are told to remember who and what we are as a Jewish nation and not to lose ourselves in the midst of the other peoples with whom we interact. The injunction to be an "***Or LaGoyim***" or a light to the nations is all about interfacing with other peoples while maintaining our "history" and past traditions, practices and teaching that define us and our present. Throughout ***Devarim/***Deuteronomy, the archetypal review lesson as the Jewish nation is poised and ready to enter their promised land of Israel, we are continually warned not to follow the ways of other peoples. While we come into contact with and interact with others and live in a world of many faiths and communities, for they too are the children of God and made in God's image, we are specifically warned to maintain a Jewish identity, a Jewish set of values and behaviors, and Jewish practices and standards. It is in this sense that the Jewish nation is to be an ***Or LaGoyim***, through unwavering and consistent obedience to God and ***remembering*** how we are supposed to live our lives.

Here too, the maintenance of the lessons and deeds of our history is not merely relegated to the word on paper, but rather dependent on our ongoing behaviors as guided and instructed by this word on paper. It is worthwhile to note that the manner in which we go through life (***ha-li-cha***) and live according to Jewish Law (***ha-la-cha***) is the same root/word in Hebrew. In this manner, we too will build a Jewish future based on the Jewish past, with memory of that past an important leg on which we build the chapters of our community yet to be experienced. It is in the ongoing implementation of this strategy that the present and future generations of children continue to observe and treasure the practices and behaviors that have been handed down by so many generations and ancestors that preceded them, though in a manner somewhat (but perhaps not that much) different from that of the Native American community.

Within this context, let us return to consider the "sixties" for just a moment. To be sure, there was rebellion and a profound testing of the values and behaviors of the "older generation" by the younger generation, thus the characteristic and identifying *generation gap* that was the subtitle of that time and its cultural context for many. What happened afterwards? There is a wonderful poster that made the rounds years, actually several decades, ago. It was entitled "The Ten Year Reunion of Woodstock." In this poster was a group of clearly upward mobile professionals in proper three piece suits carrying the obligatory briefcase, taking their place in following the paths of the generation against whom they so vehemently rebelled after all. This is definitely the picture that is worth so much more than a thousand words, to quote a well-known adage, although admittedly amended. What was the purpose of this particular rebellion? Was it to change the status quo or to become the status quo? Robert Bly points out that while children of so many generations wanted to destroy the giant at the top of Jack's beanstalk to remove the threat of his unbridled use of power, our more recent generations want to destroy the giant so that they can **become the giant**. This is an extremely different motivation in conceptualizing the purpose of rebellion as a means of social change or correction of thwarted paths taken. (27)

Each generational group has its challenges, its angst and its sense of "we have to do this for ourselves" to be sure. However, just as there is really a question as to the accuracy of the concept of the "self-made man" one has to look at such generational groupings over the longer time span as they grow and develop, not just at one point in their chronological time line. So, our generation from the sixties grew and matured and took their place in our larger community after all of their experimentation with various cultural lures and excesses. Remember that this is the precise generation that Robert Bly studies and finds them to have a difficult time setting limits and boundaries, that is, determination of the rules and regulations for the next generational grouping, too often leading to dire results.

Additionally, it is this next generation, the children of the sixties generation, that is returning to their past and often ***re-rooting*** themselves in the more stringent practices and lifestyle of several generations ago. Clearly, this is not the first time such a return to a more conventional life journey has been observed in our history. Kohelet/Ecclesiastes would remind us that this very dynamic has occurred often and frequently. Our ethnographers who study the cultural development and lives of various peoples would point to many such examples of this phenomenon in a vast variety of settings. In fact, from within a cultural context, they would claim that this disconnect and rebellion against the past is a necessary stage in each generation's mode of ownership of their individuated role in the collective continuation of the traditions and teachings that define and determine the path of their community or group.

Now, as we look today at our students for whom the sixties is their history, we are confronted once again by many questions regarding our behaviors, morals and making of healthy choices. Consider how "adult" even our children's world has become. Whereas in the fifties and early sixties, one could continue to "protect" their younger generation from the horrors and difficulties of the adult world in the United States, we as a country clearly lost our innocence as a society, many would claim, with the assassination of President John F. Kennedy as well as the soon-to-follow assassinations of Robert Kennedy and Martin Luther King Jr. For European nations and their citizenry, this loss of innocence had generally already occurred in the aftermath of World War II, if not at earlier points of contention and grievous loss.

In terms of today's world and the context in which our younger members of society are growing and learning, think of the following words: kidnap, murder, pornography, terrorism, rape, addictions, and sexual intercourse (and so many others we could include here). How many of our five to seven year old children do not know these words as well as their general meanings? It is clear that we have to bring our younger children into the reality of our tough times even earlier in the past, due in no small part to technology-aided accessibility to all that happens, regardless of age-appropriate presentation. Yet once again, a quick study of history would reveal that while the specifics of this need to be precociously mature in some elements may be characteristic to this present time and our contemporary population of youngsters, the overall phenomenon is not a new one.

Does this mean that our situation has gotten so much worse or is it possible that there is another explanation? Look at our media in which there is virtually nothing that cannot appear on screen whether in the theatre, on our televisions at home, computers or in our hand held technology. We are finding it more and more difficult to censor what is available for free viewing. We live in a culture and time and society in which the personal sex life, not to mention the questionable standards of behavior of any member of our society including our most responsible and visible leaders provides the topics for our six o'clock news daily as well as ongoing streaming and feeds that are readily available to us on our various hand held devices. The private life of our most honored leaders is everyone's business, our clergy comes under closer scrutiny due to the misdeeds of some of its members, and the sense of distance and respect from those deserving of such is virtually non-existence. Rebellion now happens on the screen in front of us 24/7. Imagine what has happened in recent years in the streets of Cairo, Ukraine, Ferguson, and so many other places as well as the visibility that it attains for all of us. Compare this to what the world must have known or not known about the Peasants' Revolt of 1381, the life in the streets of Irving Howe's world, even the lack of knowledge about what was actually happening in 1930's and 1940's Germany in other regions of the world.

Of course, this has a positive side in that we have to ask how many generations were people doing the same things and submitting others to such abuses, but able to hide under the cloak of position and authority. For example, think about when we find out that leaders in our religious communities have been acting inappropriately with people who place trust in them; and then we find out that this has been going on for years, even decades. In our culture, however, a relatively new truism is that everyone's business is, well, everyone's business. Clearly this is a technology driven phenomenon that confronts us all with the notion of "hands off" a thing of the past. Thus, the question at this point is have the behaviors of these individuals changed and devolved or are these behaviors not any different than those in the past but just more public and open?

We should remember that when we turn our clocks back and examine the public nature of life in so many other historical epochs, we would find existing phenomena and accepted standards of behavior that would truly shock us, if we were not already aware of them. Think of the outrage that the notion of institutionalized prostitution evokes in many of our modern sensibilities, yet remember how public and open it has been and continues to be in other places and spaces of our human family and the world in which we live. Similarly, Irving Howe documents the situation of several generations earlier when there were gangs on the streets, public displays of behavior that many of us do not see daily and are horrified by their existence, and other examples of normative phenomena that we would not necessarily consider to be so normative.

Consider for a moment the openness of nudity in our society. I once heard a pithy, yet profound statement quoted from a teacher of one of my children's classes, which is "pornography is a matter of geography." This is true both in terms of our horizontal community as well as geographic community. While in many African countries and communities and in so many historical periods women would habitually walk around with the top half of their body unclothed, clearly and most likely if you are reading this right now, this would not be your normal expectation in walking down the streets of your neighborhood. Pregnancy at very young ages, marriages of female children, multiple wives, public nudity, orgies, rampant use of hallucinogenic substances, gang cultures with their own brand of accepted dishonesty for a greater purpose and so many other practices, while clearly normative in so many communities and societies throughout history, are most probably not so in the one in which you, the reader, presently lives.

The point could be posited that our present moral and ethical barometer for accepted behaviors in our Western industrialized and intellectualized lives is actually higher than in previous generations and other places and spaces in history. Think about the discussions and reactions that are placed before us in all of our media sources when political leaders have affairs, when respected community members embezzle and misappropriate funds, and when our religious leaders act in a manner that is immoral and unethical. The community outrage reflects that our code of morals and ethics is not absent; quite the opposite. We react against what we consider to be an affront to our higher sense and standards of behaviors that are appropriate and those that are clearly not. We may not always be clear and certain about what the standards for those morals and ethics are, but we know that they are there. Perhaps reclaiming our past in a meaningful way as not just our history and legacy but as the blueprint of our lives would make us more sure about the foundations of these standards!

I remember being challenged by a colleague some years ago, in the mist of the various scandals surrounding President Clinton, to list all of the United States Presidents that we believed had not had affairs or acted in a manner unfaithful to their wives and family. As I recall, the list, which interested many at the time and appeared in various newspapers and magazines, was alarmingly short. Think for a moment of the carpetbaggers, culture and mores of the Roaring Twenties, medieval communities in which nudity and provocative behavior was subjected to standards quite different than those of other chapters of history including our own, the Greek gymnasia of long ago in which all sports events were done in the nude, how so many Empires were built of the foundation of perceived greatness that was based upon inhumane treatment of masses of slaves and so on. Further consider how some of these dynamics are still in play and present in our world today.

These too are most important lessons of our history, that is, our generational lives that become the history that our children study. The value of this study is so that we do not forget, and therefore hopefully do not repeat painful chapters of our past generations. The hope is that as we forge a future and walk into it ***for our own sake and the sake of our children*** as did Abraham so long ago and our own previous generations more recently, we take these lessons with us so that we remember what we are not to repeat as well as those hard earned lessons that are so critically valuable as we move on and build an even better future.

Questions for Continued Thought and Discussion:

1. What do you think has changed the most since you were a child?

2. What do you think our children will look back at and think has changed the most?

3. Which of the challenges that we confront today can you trace back to other historical periods?

4. Are there any new challenges or problems that you can identify?

5. Do you feel differently about thinking about "the good ole' days" after reading this perspective?

6. To what primary cause do you attribute the most profound changes and challenges in our lives today?

VI. Me and We

If I am not for myself, who will be for me;
If I am only for myself, what am I?

Pirke Avot/Ethics of the Fathers, Chapter 1, Mishna 14

So you think that "Me and We" is poor grammar? To be sure, it most certainly is. However, far more significant and to the point, this is reflective of the process by which we grow, we think and we learn to become part of our communities, the "we" that makes us all much stronger and more important "me's," though it may not always feel that way to us. After all, within those communities, the **we** to which we belong, may mean that some of the independence and freedom of the individual, the **me** may have to be tempered by additional boundaries and standards of the community or group of which we are part. This is clearly the case in mostly all collectives. The trick is to balance the importance and place of **me** and **we** in each of our lives in a manner that is constructive to society and simultaneously affirming to the individual.

For many years, virtually every Social Studies program that has been and often continues to be used in the beginning years of educational programming in our schools in the United States follows what is called the "expanding horizons" strategy. In this methodology, which was ever so briefly introduced earlier, we are trying to inculcate a sense of precisely this balance in our student population. That is, the youngest students in Nursery are completely focused on *ME*, that is the growth and awareness of self. Through this year and into Kindergarten, the focus shifts a bit to incorporate all of the other *ME*'s in the group. In other words, we begin to look at how we cooperate and work and think of others in our world. So much of the

Kindergarten/First Grade program is dedicated to study of family and neighborhoods – the most primary groups to which we belong.

Then as students move through the grades of Elementary School, they expand their horizons! First, in Second Grade study often turns to communities – your community, my community and many communities or *WE*'s throughout the world. At this point, students are often introduced to different cultures and peoples, their ways of life, their holidays and celebrations, and so much else as they "expand their horizons" in looking at and considering their interaction with the world. In other words, as they now have a more developed sense of self or their *ME*, they begin to focus on the groups to which we as well as others around us belong, the *WE*'s of our lives. This is another way that Bly's concerns are addressed if we can "grow our children up" correctly.

These students now move on to the complex structures and elements that compose the many facets of a functioning state, our country and finally, the world. All the while, as they are learning various skill sets (e.g. map skills, critical reading skills in learning about current events, research of primary sources, etc.) to enable them to study and consider these different groupings of which we are all part, they are also learning about the many complexities that are confronted by the many different groups in our world in interacting with each other on so many variegated levels. Further, they are exploring and acquiring problem solving and conflict resolution strategies to enable them to fully appreciate the many different aspects and facets of individual groupings and their interactions with each other. By this time, the notion that we are all members of a variety of groupings is known and understood by these students.

Critics of why Social Studies education is too often not achieving its stated goals claim that within these systems, technology, community service and other forms of participatory engagement must accompany the academic aspects of this framework. The question is what do we do with this knowledge earned skill sets, and acquired experiences; and how do we further develop it for the benefit of the individual and the group? How do we work towards the goal of building strong individuals, strong communities and the larger and stronger community of communities of which we are all members in so many different ways?

The system is a good one in that it follows the steady progression of the child as one comes of age intellectually, socially, personally and developmentally. It is hoped that through following the carefully defined steps in such an educational process while adding important experiential components, we will be sending our young leaders into our world equipped to deal with the challenges that confront them individually as well as within their various groups to which they belong. Beyond that, it is hoped that we will facilitate the involvement of whole generations of activists who will not only observe and study what is the present set of circumstances that confront them, but work to change our situation for the better in a meaningful and significant manner.

Certainly, in our world today we are so acutely aware of the many quagmires that confront us in our world as different groupings clash, be they defined religiously, politically, ethnically, racially, or by so many other possible criteria. It is too easy to be overwhelmed by the enormity of these conflicts and divisions and just walk away because, after all, what could one person possibly do to change the whole world anyway? There is a theory that we each have our own space in the world (some refer to this figuratively as "our square foot") and if we could take responsibility for that space and try to change and improve it, then we will have accomplished so much. Further, if others do the same, then think of the potential results that could be achieved. "Just imagine," as John Lennon would have us do, if we would all *adopt-a-space* (yes, like the cleaning up litter program on our highways and streets) and make that space kinder, gentler, more embracing, more focused on the power of WE.

The refrain from this chapter of "but if I am only for myself, what am I" (which is also discussed elsewhere in this collection of essays) is relevant in this understanding of the need to balance the ME and the WE and be more empowered ME's and WE's as a result of concern and connection between the group and the individual who belongs to the group. This well learned lesson is clearly evident in the Torah and can be found, among other places, in comparing the actions of Noach and Abraham regarding the groups that surround them, specifically in the responsibility of the ME towards the WE. Take note of the following two parts of the Torah narrative and a marked difference between them, which is quite significant.

First of all, in Bereshit/Genesis 6:9 – 22 we read (in part):

> These are the generations of Noach. Noach was a righteous and blameless man in his generation; Noach walked with God ... The earth became corrupt before God; the earth was filled with lawlessness. When God saw how corrupt the earth was, for all flesh had corrupted its way on earth, God said to Noach, "I have decided to put an end to all flesh, for the earth is filled with lawlessness because of them; I am ready to destroy all of them with the earth. Make for yourself an art of gopher wood: make it an ark with compartments, and cover it inside and out with pitch... For my part, I am about to bring the Flood waters upon the earth, to destroy all flesh under the sky in which there is breath of life; everything on earth will perish. But I will establish my covenant with you" ... Noach did so, just as God commanded him, this is what he did.

As we see in this story, Noach "walks with God" and was considered a "righteous and blameless man in his generation." Commentators pose the question as to whether this designation of "in his generation" should be read "for his generation." In other words, given the lawlessness and corruption of his time, by comparison he was really a great guy. It might theoretically not even have taken that much to rise to such a high position in such a social and cultural context. Clearly, even if this were to be the case, we could analyze so many different spaces and places in history and the individuals that occupy them in much the same manner.

On the other hand, as we have seen in our own world and throughout history, it is known well that when those around the ME are not observing a set standard of behaviors and moral benchmarks, it is that much more difficult for the ME to do so on their own and is therefore all the more meritorious. It is in this context that we learn the value of Hillel's statement in **Pirke Avot**/Ethics of the Fathers 2.6, in which he teaches: "In a place where there are not righteous and proper people, try to be a righteous and proper person." Here, the effort is worth so much in light of the extremely difficult challenge of the WE that would surround a specific ME. At any rate, we see that Noach was a strong ME but without impact or connection with the larger group that would be destroyed according to the text of the story. Noach does proceed to do exactly what God tells him to do, without questioning or challenging, for he did indeed "walk with God." The question we are left with, however, is why was he not engaged with and concerned about community? By not acting according to that criterion, Noach does not meet the standard set by Hillel the Elder. To be sure, this could be said about too many successful people in our history and in our world today.

Further, as Rabbi Lord Jonathan Sacks teaches, this lack of responsibility to and concern about community is ultimately to the detriment of Noach. He moves from being the man who walks with

God to the man of the soil, who becomes a drunkard. Rabbi Sacks makes the point that while Noach was righteous, he was not a leader (28). I would add the notion that Noach not being part of a community nor invested in the actions and involvements of others precluded him from even having the potential opportunity to become the leader that Rabbi Sacks values. Effective leaders have to understand and be a participating part of the collective, not just focus on their personal experience and perspective. Further, it is indeed interesting to note that in the retelling of this narrative in the Koran, Noach does show this investment in others and in fact tries to get the members of his society to worship God, or Allah (29). As the narrative is reported in the Koran, Noach is both righteous and a leader in the Muslim tradition.

Later we see a different type of situation unfold with our old friend, Avraham. At this point in the narrative, God is once again upset with the lawlessness and corruption of the citizens, this time of Sodom and Gomorrah. God questions whether or not God should tell Avraham what God is planning to do to Sodom and Gomorrah. This is unlike the directive that is immediately given, at least from the perspective of the reader, in the Noach narrative. So, God states the problem and then Avraham begins without hesitation to bargain with God, trying to save the city (i.e. the larger group) for the sake of a potentially smaller group of righteous people. In the end, this smaller group cannot be found and the cities are in fact destroyed.

We read about this in the following text from Bereshit/Genesis, chapter 18, verses 17 through 33, part of which states as follows:

> Now the Lord had said, "Shall I hide from Avraham what I am about to do, since Avraham is to become a great and populous nation and all of the nations of the earth are to bless themselves by him? For I have singled him out, that he may instruct his children and his family to keep the way of the

Lord by doing what is just and right, in order that the Lord may bring about for Abraham what God had promised him. Then the Lord said, "The outrage of Sodom and Gomorrah is so great and their sin so grave" ... Avraham came forward and said, "Will you sweep away the innocent along with the guilty? What if there should be fifty innocent within the city; will You wipe out the place and not forgive it for the same of the innocent fifty who are in it? ... And the Lord answered, "If I find within the city of Sodom fifty innocent ones, I will forgive the whole place for their sake." ... What if forty five should be found there?" And God answered "I will not destroy it, for the sake of the forty five...."

As the conversation unfolds, Avraham continues to bargain with God to save the cities for the sake of forty, thirty, twenty and then finally ten innocent souls. The problem, as we are told, is that there were not even ten righteous souls for the sake of whom the cities could be saved.

However, what is more significant here for our purposes is not so much the end of the story, as disappointing as it is, but the ongoing pleading and requests of Avraham as such a strong and impassioned ME for the sake of the citizens of Sodom and Gomorrah, the potential WE. It is even possible that there could be other than positive ramifications for Avraham's potential involvement when we carefully examine the beginning of the narrative and God's consideration as to whether or not Avraham should be told about what is to happen.

This is seen in marked contrast to the Noach story of the Torah, where Noach was concerned about the ME and the smaller grouping of his family only, while here there is concern by Avraham (the ME) for the larger grouping (the WE). This is fundamental for so many in terms of the value of the community (the WE) in Jewish thinking.

Rabbi W. Gunther Plaut explains this eloquently with few words as follows:

> Apprised of the impending destruction of Sodom and Gomorrah, Abraham rises to argue God's justice and questions [God] to [God's] face. Abraham's pleading fails not because his moral stance is faulty but because his premise is wrong: There are no righteous men in the cities.
>
> With this story it becomes clear that Abraham's religion is more than a set of cultic practices. It deals with human beings and their problems and with Abraham's faith in a God of righteousness (30).

There is also another lesson to be derived from this text regarding the importance and power of community in terms of how Jewish law roots the identification of a minimum prayer community (minyan) of ten in this text. Here the minimum size of a meaningful **WE** in the Jewish communal life is determined by Avraham in his wisdom as well as credited to his initiative on behalf of others and understanding the significance of **WE**.

Notice the difference when the individual is connected to the group and when this is not the case with regard to reciprocal concern and accountability. How is this profoundly instructive for our larger community and for our own contemporary lives? Margaret Mead's notion that citizens can accomplish through their actions what governments cannot achieve through their laws and sanctions is something that deserves serious consideration by us all. Imagine the empowerment and sense of enablement that our students would have if we educated all of them to be activists and change their "one square foot" of the world, caring for and feeling connected to those around them. This is the element that would complete and activate their understanding of expanding horizons as they mature. The good news is that this is actually happening in increasing degrees in our contemporary reality.

It is interesting today to note the prevalent growth of social entrepreneurship, which accomplishes precisely this. Individuals create entities that improve and enhance our world and its social problems outside of governmental agencies. These are dubbed by many as our **new heroes,** as they don't just ask the questions of Avraham, but take an important further step in improving the larger collectives in our world today. They certainly go well beyond the parameters of the influence of Noach.

If we can continue to enable the education and achievement of stronger and more powerful individuals, clearly the groups to which we all belong will benefit significantly. Maybe then, the Sodom's and Gomorrah's amongst us will be significantly diminished and the actions of individuals and small groups of single agents (such as the minyan of ten described above) will make incredible differences from which we all benefit, either directly or indirectly.

Further, when one considers the impact of challenges and threats to the well-being of the individual ME's amongst us, we note how the fabric of our society is threatened as well. Let's look at the sixties and seventies once again, in the context of the need to be strong ME's and the values of small groups such as the minyan and Abraham's "ten righteous people." There was clearly an alienation from the generational teachings and continued patterns that had been a source of comfort to so many during previous times at this point. In the name of individualism and in the spirit of "Don't bother me; I will do what I want," so many ME's chose freely to enter the world of drugs, alcohol, promiscuity and so many other destructive behaviors, that it further isolated many and destroyed both the significance and the power of the WE that can add so much to all of us.

In my interfaith programming work, I am asked from time to time what the significance of the need of the group is in prayer and in communal Jewish life, as this requirement we have of the presence of ten is not a necessity in other religious traditions. I am struck by the reaction when I explain how the group is needed to strengthen the individuals – that prayer, as a group experience, can be significantly more powerful than prayer offered by individuals. This actually seems somewhat counterintuitive when thinking of the pursuit of individual spiritual growth and spiritual expression of inner thoughts. Nonetheless it makes sense in a world where "peer culture," clearly a group product is understood and often valued. The collective of WE strengthens and provides focus and direction and support for the individual ME's.

As the statement at the beginning of this chapter indicated,

> If I am not for myself, who will be for me;
> If I am only for myself, what am I? (Ethics of the Fathers)

Note the clear statement of balance here. It is critically important that we become strong and well developed individual entities in order to be a constructive and contributing member of the collectives in our lives. If we do not start with a strong sense and understanding of self, then how can we be any good to others on any level?

The accountability that Robert Bly speaks about must be considered. We are not just random disconnected self-absorbed individuals floating around aimlessly as some may think that the sixties sought to indicate to us as part of its legacy, but rather integrated members of larger entities to which we all belong and from which we each ultimately benefit. Now, the challenge is to consider how we invest all of the individual members of these larger entities in the ongoing well-being of the group and the continued commitment to it. In other words, how do we follow the model set before us by Avraham in favor of the one exemplified by Noach? Only when one understands this interconnectedness between the individual and the group as well as the relationship between the various individuals within the group, will one decide to be an activist, working for the betterment and good of the group as well as on their behalf. Further, it is only at this point that one individual will understand and accept that he or she will benefit significantly from such effort and that in the end, it is clearly worthwhile to give up a bit of individual agenda and desires to become part of the larger and stronger collective that will ultimately give back support and validation to the individuals that make it a viable group.

Ironically some, if not many, would propose that this too can be found in the rebellion and rejection of the past found in the sixties and seventies. Clearly, the rebellion of the masses of individuals that characterizes that historical moment in our country achieved a group effect that was in many ways astounding and overwhelming in its own right. There are palpable changes in our social structure and in our daily lives that can clearly be attributed to this phenomenon, to the understanding of the immediacy of "if not now, when" that created such a sense of urgency during these years. Civil rights, women's rights, raising of political awareness and conscience, antiwar protests, cries for equality and so much else clearly have roots in this decade. The point could clearly be made, and indeed has by many authors and social scientists, that as a result of the rampant dissatisfaction and alienation of the individual, new group alignments were fashioned (31).

There may even be a lesson to be found in the coming together of so many individuals in this shared group experience, beyond the obvious social fabric of the time. There was, to be sure, a shared understanding that, regardless of the means used to achieve such, there needed to be changes in our society. Ultimately, it was clearly the power of the group that brought some of these changes to fruition; and it must be remembered that all of this was accomplished without the advantage and wide reach of social media that we have so readily available today.

As for now, there are many lessons to be learned from the experience of the sixties and the seventies, and yet, it could be posited that we have not passed on these lessons effectively to the next generations. Perhaps this is the legacy and result of the selfish and self-absorbed side of the change that was effected on society, as we know it, according to Bly and others. Years ago, a very frustrated and angry young man blurted out to me during a counseling meeting that I had with him, "You are so lucky. You lived through the sixties and the seventies. You knew what you stood for and what you were fighting for. Today nobody really cares anymore. I, on the other hand, am all alone. Who do I find who feels as I do?" He then went on to speak about what he knew from his parents, who are my chronological peers, about the rallies, marches, and social unrest and rebellion of that time. Citing his own concerns about how minorities are treated, growing political threats, and the general dysfunction of so much of our own society in more recent decades, he lamented that there was no group to be part of with his angst, in other words he felt lost as a ME without a WE. One could clearly make the point that this feeling is much more rampant in our troubled and fractured world today than those of us who fought those battles would like to think. Have we forgotten our history of what happens when MEs overtake WEs, only to be doomed to repeat its flawed chapters yet again?

How do we build such groups of shared agendas and sentiments? How do we instill the importance of building a constructive collective and its benefit to the individuals that bring it into being in our technologically sophisticated world that moves too fast too quickly, often leaving us psychologically and spiritually bereft? These groupings have to benefit both the larger entity and the individual simultaneously. There has to be a shared culture of empathy, a shared sense of reality and shared foundational values and beliefs. It is possible, even probable, that such groupings of the spirit and moral imperative that individuals may feel will transcend obvious lines of distinction, for example, among different collectives of ethnic origin, religious beliefs, racial identity, national interests, political beliefs, and so forth.

Consider for a moment the shared past and legacy of Jews, Christians and Muslims that unites these religious groupings profoundly as the children and nations of Avraham; juxtaposed with a history of misunderstanding, conflict, and often irreconcilable differences that is all too well known and pervasive in our contemporary reality. While it may traditionally have been more significant to create collectives exclusively along religious lines of belief and involvement, today we find ourselves often overwhelmed by the incredible differentiation between those within a defined grouping who are more fundamentalist in their beliefs and those who want to embrace others who may not believe as they do, yet are still within the faith community as defined. Separatists within any of these defined faith community groupings often have less in common with those in the same groupings who want to build these bridges with others and create cross-cultural collectives, united by shared purposes.

This is an obvious, though perhaps under-examined phenomenon that is confronting us today. Simply, new collectives are sprouting, more defined by approach to how one perceives life than the way in which one lives it. Dialogue groups, joint efforts that bring together people of different belief systems and political liaisons, inter-faith efforts, diversity programming, shared efforts of social entrepreneurship, educational programs to teach about various ethnicities and focused on having interactions with them, and other such phenomena are breaking traditional lines of collectives and their defined terms of belonging. There is increasing movement towards the notion that we need to reconnect as the largest WE, that is, as members of the family of humanity in the face of so much in our world and our history that is significantly less than humane. This is the family of which we read in the beginning of the Torah, which forms foundational elements of the Tanach/Jewish Bible, the Old and New Testament, and Koran, as well as other developed narratives that are held onto by various faith communities.

In a time when we are talking about "***When Religion Becomes Evil***" with the help of authors such as Charles Kimball and reading and hearing about the violent reactions groups have to each other as part of our daily "news at six" fare, and in other ways being bombarded about the black side of that which is supposed to heal; it is all the more poignant and necessary to look at what unites us as people of faith, belief and shared hopes. We must remember what foundational values are shared by the larger collective and then distilled into the various religious interpretations that we all hold on to in our personal lives. National, ethnic, racial and other identities are to be preserved in all of their integrity for this is who each of the ME's among us is. At the same time, we must learn to share what is special and unique about us with each other, not judge and exclude the "other" because he or she is not part of the defined exclusive collective to which we belong. It is in this way that we will all be the strongest individuals possible while also working in a constructive manner to build strong collectives in our larger social and cultural family of humanity in a humane way.

Questions for Continued Thought and Discussion:

1. In a few sentences, write your own reaction to the question "If I am not for myself, who will be for me?"

2. What are the positive aspects of focusing on self over group?

3. What are the negative aspects of focusing on self over group?

4. What are the positive aspects of focusing on group over self?

5. What are the negative aspects of focusing on group over self?

6. How can YOU achieve the balance in YOUR life between ME and WE?

VII. Values and Actions

A man came to Shammai and Hillel, each in turn. He explained that he would convert if the entire Torah could be taught to him while he stood on one foot. Shammai sent him away, chasing him with a measuring stick to indicate his displeasure with the request. Hillel listened to the man's challenge and said to him, "Do not do unto the other what you would not want him to do unto you. The rest of the Torah is commentary; now go and learn it." The man converted to Judaism.

Talmud: Shabbat 31a

One of my favorite segments of Talmud comes from Sotah 14b, quoted elsewhere in these essays. In it we read about how one "walks with God." The text goes on to explain that in "walking with God" we cannot just see and have a chat, so to speak, with God but rather, we act as God does. In so doing, we show our valuing of our religious souls and God's presence through our actions. This is not a platitude, but rather a practical application, which pervades everyday actions in our everyday lives. Just as involvement with and service to community gives life to the "expanding horizons" learning schematic as discussed in an earlier essay, so too our actions bring our values to life.

In the discussion that is presented in the text from Sotah, several concrete examples of such actions are indicated as we have noted earlier. It is explained that God clothed Adam and Eve in the Garden of Eden. In following the example set as God did this for people, we too are to cloth the naked – to provide for those in need to the best of our ability. Next, as the text continues, we are informed that God visited Avraham when he was recovering from his circumcision. From this we learn the value of the **_mitzvah_** of visiting those who are ill. God also comforted Yitzchak when he was mourning the loss of his parents, Avraham and Sarah. So we are to follow this example and comfort those who are mourning losses in our own community. Finally, in this text it is shown that God buried **Moshe Rabbeinu**/Moses when he died. So we should also bury our dead with respect and love. These deeds and actions are called in Hebrew **Hesed** or deeds of kindness and caring. As God performs them, we should emulate God in bringing them into our own lives and this is the manner in which one walks with God throughout one's daily life and actions. It is here that Harold Kushner's statement "Human beings are God's presence in this world" rings so true in a visceral manner.

One of the truly remarkable aspects of Judaism is that we are ordered or commanded to do these nice deeds of kindness and caring, these deeds of **Hesed**. This is indicated in the introductory text for this chapter and is one of our most critical foundational principles. Further, it must be stated that this is not the same as our American culture in which it is nice to be so considerate of others and do such things. If we volunteer to make such efforts in our American community, this is particularly noteworthy. By contrast, however, the Jewish system of living indicates that such actions are necessary for the very preservation of society every *me* is dictated to have such ongoing investment in the larger *we*. Jews are required by Jewish law to do these things according to the dictates that define the parameters for this way of life. These actions are part of our rules and regulations, those instructions that structure our society and balance the needs and freedoms of the individual and the community! What an important statement about the fundamental values of this people through these required actions!

Further, these actions are commanded both within the grouping of the Jewish people as we are to show love for fellow Jews or ***Ahavat Yisrael*** as well as in our dealings with and amongst all members of the human family in a variety of instances, as we observe the prescribed action of loving the members of our human family, known as *Ahavat Olam*. Once again, we see the marked difference taught about how we are to relate to the larger group in terms of our stories of Noach and Avraham from our previous chapters. While it might be noteworthy to be so, it is simply not enough to be righteous for one's own sake and in one's own self-interest. Rather, in following the example set by Avraham, we are to be righteous and do proper things within our investment in and concern for the group of which we are a part as well. In so doing, our worth as individuals is enhanced significantly as is our sense of purpose in our world. In these connections, our commanded values and actions as Jews are critical elements of the larger equation of humanity and our part in it. Here the individual is not as valuable alone as he or she is as part of the group.

This is the lesson that Hillel wants to teach the potential convert as well as all of us in the short text indicated in the beginning of this chapter. Of course, the details and the laws and the specifics of how one lives a Jewish life are important and relevant, and therefore must be learned and understood. However, if one does not comprehend the foundational principals upon which this way of life is based; then we must ask what the point of the system and its many details are to the individual or to the group to which the individual belongs.

There is a fairly well known story that is told in our *Musar* tradition about a Rabbi (Rebbe) who invited his students to his Shabbat table for a festive meal. The Rabbi's wife had been working hard for many, many hours to prepare this fine feast in a way that would reflect the appropriate honor she held for her husband and his scholarly students. As they were all standing around the beautiful table set with the finest china, crystal and the many special objects that will further enhance the honoring of Shabbat, the Rabbi begins to intone the words of **Kiddush**, sanctifying the meal and to be followed by the drinking of the wine.

In the meantime, among the many specific details involved in the preparation of such a feast, it is customary to cover the **Hallah** (the special bread eaten on Shabbat and Jewish Holidays) with an appropriate covering, one that is often elaborately decorated, so as not to "embarrass" the **Hallah** while we are making such a big deal about the wine as we bless and drink it. Now, obviously this is symbolic and as is the case with so much of Jewish observance and practice, such object lessons are clearly intended to teach us much larger lessons.

As the Rabbi moves through his recitation of the **Kiddush**, he notices that a very tiny corner of the **Hallah** is "peeking" out and not properly covered. As he continues to recite this important and meaningful prayer, it is obvious that he is growing angrier and angrier by the moment. Finally the **Kiddush** is completed, all drink from their cups, curious about what could be so wrong and then it happens. The Rabbi lashes out in public at his wife about how could she have been so negligent to not make sure that the **Hallah** was properly covered.

Obviously, the point of the story is that this Rabbi, for all of his learning and scholarship, did not understand the "object lesson" of covering the **Hallah**. For if we are so concerned to protect the feelings of a specified concoction of flour, eggs and water, should we not be all the more careful to protect and watch how we can and do have a profound impact upon the feelings of those that can actually be insulted, embarrassed, or hurt!

In Judaism and in Jewish Law, as we have already discussed, there are two categories of **Mitzvot** or commanded actions. There are those that are prescribed for the relationship between man and God –

Mitzvot bein Adam LaMakom – and those that are prescribed for the interactions of man and man – *Mitzvot bein Adam LeChavero*. Both are operative in a synchronistic manner in our communities as we continually interface with others while bringing God into our world through our proper actions.

We are often taught in our many codes of laws of Jewish living to be sure that we do not embarrass another human being; for if one does so, they are also hurting or insulting the very essence of that person, who is none other than God. For after all, if God is at the core of each of us, made in the image of God or **BeTzelem Elokim**, then there is no way to show disrespect or disregard for that which God has created without showing the same to God as well. As we learn in **Pirke Avot 4.1**, "Who is the one worthy of honor? The one who honors a fellow human being." In the Talmud, while there are many injunctions against embarrassment of another in **Baba Metzia 58b**, to cite one example, such embarrassment is compared to bloodshed, clearly a most horrendous and profoundly disturbing misdeed.

In our maintaining of this standard in our relations with others, it is clear that there is often virtually no distinction between and certainly much overlap among those commanded actions and established standards of behavior between us and God, and those governing actions amongst ourselves. We speak both of the sanctity and honor of God (**Kibbud HaShem**) and the sanctity and honor of all those created by God, (**Kibbud HaBeriot**). In fact, the point could be made (and Harold Kushner and others certainly have) that it is precisely through these actions of caring, empathy and so much else amongst ourselves that we best interact with God. We learn, for example, in Rambam's **Hilchot Tefillah** in his **Mishnah Torah** that it is preferable for us to pray with others than alone whenever possible, so here while beseeching and communicating with God, we are to continue to be part of and mindful of community and how the *me* and *we* amplify and bring more respect and notice to each other through our collective and shared actions and involvements.

Further, we are taught that if we commit any infractions in private that are less than honest because we think that no one is watching or sees what we are doing, and the community or an individual, including the one committing the infraction, is harmed (think of Achan in the Book of Joshua as we discussed in Chapter 4) this is even more egregious for how is it possible that God is no one? Therefore, the standards that we must apply to our actions and involvements must be consistent and in operation 24/7 for that is the amount of time we are accompanied by The One Who Created us. While this is an ideal that is difficult, if not impossible, to argue with from the vantage point of understanding the foundational elements of Judaism, the reality is that way too often this is not the way many interpret their Jewish lives according to Jewish law.

For example, within the Jewish community today, there is a grouping generally within the Reconstructionist movement who specifically feels that too many of our individual Jewish community members have become so enveloped by the details of the ritualistic aspects of our lives, such as covering the *Hallah* in the story just cited, that they have lost the essence of the meaning of such practices in the lessons they hold for us in our treatment of each other and in our obligation to build and be accountable to community. In light of this disconnect, this grouping has articulated a strategy for living and acting entitled *Values Based Decision Making*. This methodology is intended as a response to, among other things, the overemphasis of the ritualization of Jewish practice amongst many observant Jews, what is perceived by some as their sometimes much too narrow and myopic reading of elements of the sources and texts that inform our lives, and the disconnect of that emphasis from the rules and regulations and clearly articulated values that are also based in Jewish Law. These rules and regulations and values do in fact govern our everyday actions and interactions with others, providing as much detail and instruction as the dictates involved with ritual practices do, and often more so. To be sure, this is not the first time this has happened in the Jewish world, and yet it appears that once again, we as a collective have not yet learned our lesson. We have, as cited earlier, forgotten our history and are unfortunately repeating well-honed mistakes.

Moving backwards a bit in our Jewish History Timeline, the ***Musar*** movement founded within the confines of the religiously observant and accountable community itself and dedicated to a very similar agenda, began in the nineteenth century and became an important and compelling voice, one which was so difficult for many adherents to hear. Its main premise was that ***Halacha*** or Jewish Law was rooted and founded within the strictest standards of ethical behavior. Further in being accountable to society and one's community, this would not only benefit others but the individual person who accepted such responsibility in insuring that he or she would not become unduly preoccupied with one's own self-interest and ego to the exclusion of others. The ***Musar*** movement truly presented an important synthesis and interfacing of the commanded actions as well as the dictated ethical standards that was to encourage social justice as much as learning, and caring for others as much as dedication to one's own religiously framed life.

Clearly, this was ***Values Based Decision Making*** in its own right, based upon the texts and sources that informed the very being of Jewish community. Pulling on the message of the Later Prophets from our Tanach/Jewish Bible, the notion was originally that this movement was to provide the ethical template for the entirety of the Jewish community, its leaders and its members. However, due to the needs of the time, it became a code for personality training of individual members who needed to be reminded of the intrinsic balance in Jewish living between serving God and constructively serving community and self in doing so. The awe one was to have for God and sense of regard for self and others had somehow become lost in the details of the fabric of Jewish life for too many of its adherents, who tried to regain this balance in their lives. Clearly the need for such in individual lives, and meaningful reminder of this balance remains in our larger Jewish community until today. As we have already discussed, it is clearly a challenge in other faith communities as well. All would do well to remember that the first narrative of Torah reminds us that every being and element is created by God, and that the human being is specifically fashioned in the image of God ever so carefully.

There have been many, in fact too many, times throughout our Jewish history where this message had to be repeated yet again in the face of a loss of sense of balance between rituals and the ethics they were to represent and teach through observance and adherence to them. Consider the message of our Later Prophets, who continually had to remind the Jewish people during the period of the Kings or the **Malchut Yisrael** that God was so angered and dismayed by this loss of understanding that God had to prescribe as well as maintain a difficult and painful distance between God, the very source of ethics and behaviors, and the people God so loved.

In Jeremiah, chapter 5, verses 26 – 29, we read this most painful diatribe, so representative of this tone of these prophets of social justice and **Ethical Monotheism**:

> For among My people are found wicked men, who lurk, like fowlers lying in wait; they set up a trap to catch men. As a cage is full of birds, so their houses are full of guile; that is why they have grown so wealthy. They have become fat and sleek; they pass beyond the bounds of wickedness and they prosper. They will not judge the case of the orphan, not give

a hearing to the plea of the needy. Shall I not punish such deeds, says The Lord.

In Isaiah, we find a similarly painful sentiment in such passages as this one found in Chapter 1, verses 11 – 18, in which God specifically tells the Jewish Nation to cease all ritual observances, as they are meaningless without the accompanying proper actions with and towards each other.

> "What need have I of all your sacrifices?" says God. "I am sated with burnt offerings of rams, and hard parts of fatlings and blood of bulls; and I have no delight ... that you come to appear before Me. Who asked that of you? Trample My courts no more. Bringing oblations is futile. Your incense is offensive to Me. New moons and Sabbath, proclaiming of solemnities ... fill me with loathing. They are a burden to Me; I cannot endure them. And when you lift up your hands I will turn My eyes away from you; though you pray at length, I will not listen. Your hands are stained with crime; wash yourselves clean and put your evil doings away from My sight. Cease to do evil and learn to do good. Devote yourselves to justice, aid the wronged, uphold the fights of the orphan and defend the cause of the widow.

Throughout the Later Prophets, this painful message and the reality it represents is repeated too many times. The point was clearly not that God did not want the Jewish Nation to come and observe the prescribed rituals and be accountable to God through their worship, absent proper behavior and actions towards each other. Rather, God acknowledged, in these texts, the inherent hypocrisy of their ongoing appeal to God, while not attending to their social responsibility and obligation in caring for and being concerned with each other. This was a most serious flaw and had to be corrected first. Then as a cleansed and understanding people, it was hoped that the Jewish

Nation would and could return to their Temple and festival celebrations and observances. This was the intended goal. Only through a full understanding of the inextricable connection that was to join ritual and ethical deed would both elements as well as each category of *mitzvot* achieve their desired purpose.

Clearly, the problem was that the intended connection between the ritual and its meaning and the behaviors that are supposed to be representative of foundational ethics was not there. We are taught in our sources that the purpose of commanded actions and behaviors, our *Mitzvot u'Midot*, is specifically to refine us, as we are taught in **Genesis Rabbah 44.1**, for example. Obviously and unfortunately, this system did not nor does it always work in this intended manner. As we have noted, this should not be seen as a critique of the system per se, but rather as a result of adherents who freely choose to define what they are supposed to do and take control that is not theirs to take.

Rabbi Jonathan Sacks and Charles Kimball are just two of so many authors that write extensively about this abuse and the disturbing consequences that obtain from such abuse. It is indeed interesting and of great concern to note that in a community so dedicated to doing things in the proper and prescribed manner, such a profound disconnect can exist. Further, we see only three of the many periods of our history in which this same dynamic presented here, indicating a consistent pattern of the presentation of this same challenge and resulting threat to the well-being of all members of the Jewish nation, both individually and collectively. Certainly, moderate and genuinely sincere leaders and practitioners of Christianity and Islam who observe a similar discordance in their own traditions are likewise disappointed and overcome by angst as systems that are inherently so potentially positive and healing can be grossly misused and abused by adherents. To be sure, we could make the same case for other religious groupings as well. This dynamic and its pervasive presence in our world is evidenced in the relatively recent proliferation of writings within these various communities expressing ideas remarkably similar to those contained here as well as in our daily news from around the world.

Such situations of extremism being the operative prism through which religion is viewed and shared is the polar opposite of what is taught in the text in Sotah and by Hillel to the potential convert who came to him in search of truth and a way of life as described in the beginning of this chapter. Here we are so many centuries later still facing the very same struggle and the dire consequences that too often evolve as a result. If we were successful in understanding this fundamental connection in our lives between the ritual actions and the foundational values of our religious traditions and communities, clearly Charles Kimball's When Religion Becomes Evil would not be the important and painful statement it is in our world today, resonating so loudly and clearly for the many who have come to suspect the institution of religion at least and loathe it at most. Further, one cannot help but notice the correlation between this dynamic and the decreasing numbers of self-identified persons of faith in contemporary studies and reports such as those that are produced by the PEW foundation.

What has gone so terribly wrong? Rabbi Israel Salanter, the identified father of the *Musar* movement briefly mentioned above, wrote extensively in the middle of the nineteenth century about the very same problems that the Later Prophets lamented, as referenced earlier. He explained how members of the Jewish people needed to return to the fundamental values and ethics on which their lives were based and remember to be honest in their business dealings, careful with their words and speaking with each other, and forthright in all matters of daily life. This, he taught, along with so many others, was foundational in living a Jewish life (32).

In support of this same balanced diet of religious observance, in Masechet Yoma in the Babylonian Talmud, on 86a, we read as follows:

> One should read Torah, learn the Mishna and act accordingly towards Torah scholars, and all of his business and social dealings with people should be conducted in a pleasant and appropriate manner. What do people say about such a person? Fortunate is the parent who teaches him Torah; fortunate is the teacher who teaches him Torah; how unfortunate it is for those who do not learn Torah… See how pleasant are his ways and how refined are his deeds… But for the one who learns Torah, studies Mishna and acts accordingly towards Torah scholars and his business dealings are not conducted with faith and whose speech with others is not pleasant and appropriate; what do people say about that one? Woe unto his father who taught him Torah, woe unto his teachers who taught him Torah, this person who learned Torah, see how horrible are his deeds and how ugly are his ways.

In the context of the Gemara discussion, this is seen as a *Hillul HaShem*, a profanation of the name of God in the most fundamental and injurious way. Salanter understood this all too well and went so far as to strongly suggest that a portion of the weekly Shabbat be set aside for precisely this study of the need for balance of proper actions in our daily lives and interactions with each other alongside our ritual observances and study of sacred texts. The *Musar* movement was all about challenging ourselves to build community and to act in a way in which the good of the collective is well served. In other words, the honest and consistent valuing of community was and is part of our foundational beliefs as a people. Here we see a reprise of that idea of giving up a bit of me for the betterment of the we in which all associated me's are ultimately strengthened.

The obvious dilemma to address is what if everyone in our various communities of which we are part does not buy into this idea? This is most certainly not a hypothetical intellectual exercise, for clearly we know that this is the case in our daily reality. The greatest challenge of all is to try to understand or appreciate the view and position of someone with whom you disagree. This is the true test of building community; can we co-exist with our different and variant points of view and orientations within our different groupings of which we are part? Further, how do we, and is it even possible to, include those who do not subscribe to such thinking within our community building efforts? It is no different than the kindergarten goal of teaching all of the different children to play nicely on the same playground. However, the stakes in our adult world are clearly higher to be sure, for if we do not learn this skill, there may very well be no playground on which to play at all, so to speak. This threat is becoming more real and present every day in our contemporary lives.

I will be the first one to state how difficult a goal this is. Some years ago, I was involved in such a situation of conflicted understandings and was trying to see and validate the perspective of the other individual, carefully listening to their point of view. Simultaneously, I was sharing various ideas and aspects of how I understood a particular situation that had transpired and attempting to elicit the other's understanding of my perspective. The individual simply did not want to listen to my point of view after expressing their own, and cut me off immediately by stating, "it's all water under the bridge." Further, the individual would not engage in the attempt for resolution that I had placed before this person.

I realized soon after this conversation that this blithe comment that was quoted is a highly overrated saying that not one that necessarily serves the purpose of shared understanding and the building of communities of communities – perhaps, this is yet another hallmark of our hallowed American culture for too many. It may work for a behavioral aberration or an isolated misunderstanding, but it is **not** an explanation or excuse for an established pattern of one's modus operandi in not working to build community or to have empathy and understanding for the other, with whom one may rightfully disagree. One who ascribes to the saying "it's all water under the bridge" does not have to deal with accountability or address consequences of their ongoing actions. That is, one who lives by this philosophy does not necessarily need to consider the impact and effects of one's actions, one's free choice on another in a deliberate and purposeful manner.

By contrast, Judaism **commands** us to live carefully, gently, intentionally and thoughtfully. How we treat each other always matters, we are always accountable for our actions as well as the values that inform them, and they are **never** water under the bridge, so to speak. For example, consider the simple saying that every American child learns:

> Sticks and stones will break my bones;
> But names will never hurt me.

As we have already seen, our Talmud does not hold that this is a valid maxim. The Jewish standards of **Shmirat HaLashon** or that body of laws that structure how we speak to each other takes a completely different and opposite approach. "Death and life are at the hands of the tongue" as we learn in **Mishlei/**Proverbs (18:21). Notice must be taken of the order of this verse, indicating that our speech can have powerful, even dire effects. In a moment in time where everyone hears about and is acutely aware of bullying on so many levels and the profound damage it brings, we must remember that the sword of words is as powerful as any other implement in inflicting lasting and irreparable harm on others. We are adjured here and elsewhere to think before we speak and to do so with purpose and concern; in fact we are **commanded** to do so in entire codes of Jewish law dedicated to this topic alone. As already indicated, the body of laws and dictates governing our speech certainly rivals the collection of laws regarding any number of ritual aspects of our lives as Jews. The same truth holds for our dealings in business, in our familial relationships and so much else that is related to our normative behaviors during the course of the day.

It is worth noting that in Jewish educational circles, there is often talk of the dual rootedness of our value system that is shared by our Jewish and American thought systems and body of law. Yet, here we see that there is not always a shared culture, and in these instances, Jewish law may require more of us, in fact, **demand** actions and initiatives that would not otherwise be required within our American community. When these differences reflect foundational elements of the soul of what it is to be a Jewish member of a Jewish grouping, we cannot ignore such standards.

Consider that so much of the Talmud, the authoritative treatise that expounds extensively on the rules and regulations that govern our lives, is profoundly dedicated to such matters. It has always been a powerful statement to me that in so many, if not most, instances when Talmud is taught to students in our Jewish Day Schools and other educational institutions, the first text of this extensive work that is learned is from **Baba Matzia**, the section of Jewish law dedicated to what one does when one finds lost property and how one must declare the property that one has found. Why is it that before so many discussions of ritual practices that are characteristically part of a Jewish person's life, do we teach and learn about the requirement of making an honest attempt to return lost property to its rightful owner, observing the commandment of **Hashevat Aveidah**? Further, every part of this discussion about declaring lost property and attempting to find the owner and one's responsibility to do what is correct and required in such instances is so different from the little philosophy from our childhood rooted in American culture that states "finders keepers, losers weepers." Imagine how much would change on our children's playgrounds and in our adult business offices, not to mention in the daily opportunities we all have to exercise a positive impact on the lives of others with whom we come in contact if we were to **really and intentionally** observe these aspects of Jewish law with the same sense of urgency and scrupulous attention to detail that so many readily bring to ritual practices.

To be sure, there is a critically important lesson here about the essence of Jewish living and law. Real Judaism and Jewish living is nothing less than a 24/7 matter. With all due respect, **Shabbat** and **Kashrut** and other ritual aspects of this way of life are, comparatively speaking, the "easy stuff" of Jewish life! How we treat each other, ethical actions in business transactions, our scrupulous behaviors in all matters of daily interactions, the careful choice and use of our words, and so much else --- this is the real test of how one adheres to this system of living. This was the message of the Later Prophets – fail at these actions and the rituals are not worth what they should be and do not carry their intended meaning or affect. We must begin with valuing ourselves, each other, and the collective groups of which we are part; and then, and only then will we have the attention and approval of God, if that is indeed what we seek.

Taking care of our own "square foot of space," being apt representatives of what is good and just, and living the connection between our values and actions are all required just as much, if not more so than the myriad of details that define our lives ritualistically. Think of how powerful we could be in launching a "Religion is Ethical Behavior" campaign in which all peoples and groupings of faith would be held accountable in such actions as honesty, understanding, acceptance of others, compassion and so much else as **required actions** of people of faith. In addition to the obvious healing effect this would most certainly have on our world, it would be the best offensive one could take in fighting the "bad name" that religion has acquired in too many instances in the electrically charged circumstances in which we presently live. In such a world, no religious Jew could claim that "embezzlement is not prohibited in the Torah" and any person worried about protecting the feelings of flour and water would clearly value the feelings of those who can shed tears and experience laughter. This is a noble goal for all peoples of faith, to be sure – the understanding that we are **obligated** to act in such a manner at all times and in all instances.

Questions for Continued Thought and Discussion:

1. What is your understanding of what Hillel said to the potential convert in the beginning of this chapter?

2. Why do you think there is this conflict between ritual practices and those that are mandated in our relationships with others in our world?

3. How would you respond to someone who would say that you should focus on your relationship to God more than how others feel?

4. What do you think is the most important message of this chapter?

VIII. Passion or Compassion

These are the things you are to do: Speak the truth to one another, render true and perfect justice in your gates. And do not contrive evil against one another, do not love perjury; because all those are things that I hate, declares the Lord.

Zechariah 8: 16 - 17

Once again, our Later Prophets reemphasize the message that may very well seem repetitive to us by now, but somehow still needs to be conveyed given the circumstances of our reality. This "outtake" of the Biblical prophetic voice, as is the case with the others that are quoted earlier, is accompanied by God's painful declarations that we should not come to our Temple with prayers and offerings if this is the way that people will continue to act in their daily lives. When one considers the history of religion and the too often violent and devastating clashes of different faith groupings, too many amongst us are left at a loss for words of justification and praise for the institution of religion.

As one respected colleague of mine who constantly wrestles with his own religious identity often comments in a general as well as specific manner, "I see the passion, but where is the compassion?" As painful a question, and its implicit statement, this is for the person who says it, it is equally difficult and unsettling for a person of faith to hear it and acknowledge the truth and devastation that motivates it. How can the system that is based upon the bringing of comfort and support to its adherents result in the absolutely opposite effect too often? What does this say about the system itself and the values and ethics on which it is based? Or alternatively, as we have explored in these writings, what does this show us about the people who adhere to such a system and its dictates?

Ironically enough, in a brief aside, it is poignant to note that *com-* as a prefix of a word means "with" or "together." So the word *compassion* actually means "with passion." This is indeed a valuable concept to consider; that as *people of compassion we are to act with passion.* Remember the important lesson, cited earlier, that God actually prays that God will always be able to act with compassion in all dealings with people. The problem is that when you remove the *com-* prefix, passion has too often been without compassion. This is an important point in Kimball's treatise, is clearly reflected in the very sound of the legal term "crime of passion," and is something to consider when examining the history of the presentation of Passion Plays in the Christian community throughout its history. This last element has been brought back to the forefront of our collective conscience with the release some years ago of a movie that tells the story of The Passion in the Christian community, while having evoked a myriad of different reactions in other communities.

Certainly, through the Crusades, the ongoing battles between Islam and Christianity, the multitude of religious wars fought on every one of our continents and in so many other instances in every century, we see people of faith use (some would posit that they misuse) their passion, devoid of compassion. Clearly, this was the fear and complaint of the Prophets of Social Justice, so important and critical to the continued legacy and history of the Jewish nation. Additionally, this message can be found in Jesus' words as well as in the text sources of Islam and within other religious systems leading to remarkably similar conclusions about desired goals.

To take just a few examples consider these texts from the New Testament and Qu'ran, respectively:

In the Book of Matthew we learn as follows (33):

> If you then, who are evil, know how to give good gifts to your children, how much more will your Father who is in heaven give good things to those who ask him! So whatever you wish that men would do to you, do so to them, for this is the law and the prophets." (7: 11 – 12)

With respect to context, it is important to remember that this text, while adjuring adherents to strive to be the best, acknowledges that all come from the beginning of Original Sin and are inherently riddled with that which is not good. This is a profound difference between such adages in the New Testament and the Tanach. Nonetheless, the values that are espoused remain so fundamentally similar.

A second text comes to us from Colossians:

> Put on then, as God's chosen ones, holy and beloved, compassion, kindness, lowliness, meekness, and patience, forbearing one another and if one has a complaint against another, forgiving each other; as the Lord has forgiven you, so you also must forgive. And above all these put on love, which binds everything together in perfect harmony. (3: 12 – 14)

Notice again, that these values and characteristics, actually defined earlier as ***midot*** are familiar to us from the chapters and verses of the Tanach, the Old Testament to the New Testament.

The Qu'ran, like the Tanach, stresses that it is not precision and perfection in ritual observance (here represented by "turn[ing] your faces to the East and to the West"), but rather living with compassion and caring for others in our daily actions and deeds that is the pious life (34). Clearly the prophets of social justice would approve of this.

> It is not [for] piety, that you turn your faces to the East and to the West. True piety is this: To believe in God, and the Last Day, the angels, the Book, and the Prophets, to give of one's substance, however cherished, to kinsmen and orphans, the needy, the traveler, beggars, and to ransom the slave, to perform the prayer, to pay the alms. And they who fulfill their covenant, when they have engaged in a covenant, and endure with fortitude, misfortune, hardship and peril, these are they who are true in their faith, these are the truly [G]od-fearing. (Al Quran 2: 172 - 174)

As a second example from the Qu'ran, consider this text that is part of the weekly sermon on Fridays:

> And we have sent down [to you] the Book, making clear everything, and as a guide and a mercy, and as good tidings to those who surrender. Surely God bids to justice and doing good and giving to kinsmen: and God forbids indecency, dishonor, and insolence, admonishing you, so that you will remember. This is fulfilling God's covenant... (Al Qu'ran 16: 92 – 93)

To seek the path of peace, to bring healing to the world and to otherwise work for the collective good of all of humanity with ***compassion*** is clearly an important and critical ideal in each of these traditions. Unfortunately, however, it is too often compromised and threatened by our religiously motivated passion when it gets in the way. How do we address this threat to our family of humanity while maintaining the integrity of our various systems of religious life? How ironically sad it is that the very hope and ideal we share in trying to achieve the best of what we can become is the downfall that plagues too many in all of our communities of faith.

Returning to the Tanach for just a moment, in Micah, yet another one of the Prophets of Social Justice, chapter 6, verse 8, we read:

> What does God require from you: To do justice, love goodness, and to walk humbly with your God.

These are seemingly simple words to be sure and encapsulate the more verbose quotes indicated earlier as well as many more statements and formulas found in this genre of Biblical literature. Who can argue with such a simple yet clearly profound sentiment? Clearly, these words, as so many others that carry the same message, resonate with all monotheistic traditions that have developed and look back to these very sources for inspiration and instruction.

Let us examine this picture and see what we can discern in terms of where the passion is and where the compassion can be found and the degree to which they must interface with and temper each other. For purposes of this examination, let us make a distinction between mainstream religion and extreme fundamentalism. Let us also propose that within every religious continuum there is a fundamentalist component that does not necessarily reflect the vast majority of the expression of that religious tradition within its mainstream. Further within fundamentalist streams, there will characteristically be an over-exaggeration of some religious maxims while others in the same system will be compromised or obliterated altogether within this exaggeration. In this loss of balance, many of the teachings just shared will actually be eclipsed by the religious fervor so many of our prophets and teachers of old eschew.

It is this type of focus that explains how extremely Orthodox Jews in certain neighborhoods may throw garbage at other Jews as they walk through their defined communities. It is this orientation that leads extreme Fundamentalist Christians to claim that they alone know what God wants and accepts and therefore have permission to persecute and destroy others who do not share their beliefs. Further, this perspective provides some adherents of Islam with the notion that they can assume absolute control over their women in a manner that much of the civilized world (as we know and experience it) would claim violates their human rights or obliterate so many human lives through suicide bombings, including members of their own faith community.

Consider that one leader of an American white supremacist organization, a woman who has been interviewed and profiled from time to time on television magazine shows, has continually used all available forms of media to publicly state and reiterate that the agenda and teachings of the Ku Klux Klan, Christianity, and living a good and moral life are synonymous with each other. Clearly, the harmful ramifications of schooling and nurturing generations of children with this thinking as their foundational template as this woman and others do daily, all in the name of their faith, are obvious. This statement and its problematic implications are obvious for mainstream Christianity, and even more so for the other traditions that have been indicated here, as well as for the racial, ethnic, national and general mix that comprises our larger American and world community.

John Adams, one of the founding fathers of that larger American community, is reported to have publicly thanked the Jewish brethren within the larger community for teaching and showing all how to be a more civilized and caring community, according to a variety of historical accounts. As he wrote in a letter to Francois Adriaan van der Kemp in February of 1809:

> **I will insist that the Hebrews have done more to civilize men than any other nation. If I were an atheist, and believed in blind eternal fate, I should still believe that fate had ordained the Jews to be the most essential instrument for civilizing the nations.** If I were an atheist of the other sect, who believe or pretend to believe that all is ordered by chance, I should believe that chance had ordered

the Jews to preserve and propagate to all mankind the doctrine of a supreme, intelligent, wise, almighty sovereign of the universe, which I believe to be the great essential principle of all morality, and consequently of all civilization (35).

Clearly these teachings are the ideals of the Later Prophets, as they reflect the words and dictates of Torah, which are found throughout the sources so representative of our monotheistic traditions as well as others. What happened so that these very ideals and instances in which God clearly indicated that to observe the ritualistic aspects without these components was unacceptable have been forgotten, or worse, ignored by a whole segment of our religious communities, such as that exemplified by the woman referenced here? Many would propose that it is precisely this imbalance that most divides the fundamentalist and mainstream segments of our religious communities and that in many ways, those within the mainstream of their respective religious groupings have more in common with each other across denominational and religious divides than they do with their fundamentalist counterparts within their own religious communities.

For example, it is within the mainstream of the monotheistic religions that one finds the most dialogue about shared traditions, hopes and teaching of compassion, that is the ideals and teachings of the Later Prophets and their rootedness in Torah, recognized as the beginnings for Christianity and Islam as well as Judaism. It is within these mainstream groupings that one finds people that are often willing to sit down and learn about the differences as well as share what is characteristic of each of the traditions. The values of loving one's neighbors, caring for those who are not as fortunate as others in the community and the other standards of collective self-interest for the sake of community are all benchmarks to uphold for so many adherents, clearly the majority in each of these faith groupings.

Sadly, there is also a shared pain regarding the extremist readings of the same texts that would dictate other than these ideas. It is here that the compassion for which my colleague is seeking is found.

It is most interesting to note that the very maxim of the importance of saving a life because it is equal to the saving of an entire world appears in almost identical wording in both the Talmud for the Jewish faith community and in the Qu'ran.

Note the following texts:

> Whoever destroys a soul, it is considered as if he destroyed an entire world. And whoever saves a life, it is considered as if he saved an entire world. (Mishna Sanhedrin 4:9)
>
> The taking of one innocent life is like taking all of Mankind ... and the saving of one life is like saving all of Mankind" (Al Qur'an, 5:33).

Yet, in both communities, we do find antithetical teachings about war and the purposes it will achieve in spreading the absolute truths that Fundamentalists will hold. It is these teachings, often taken out of context and as singular dictates, that will inspire a Baruch Goldstein, or Muslim suicide bomber or a White Extremist who claims that the Ku Klux Klan, Christianity, and the love of God are one and the same. Here is where we might want to wonder where the passion lost its compassion. How do we insure that this balance, as all others indicated here, is maintained in a meaningful and constructive manner in the spirit of the religious tradition in which it is rooted?

Rabbi Jonathan Sacks speaks at length about potentially challenging texts. He explains that we all have them and that interpretation and understanding the context of such texts is critical before inappropriate extrapolation and use of them to justify behaviors that are self-serving and antithetical to the original intent of our respective Holy Writs. He cautions as follows:

> Every text-based religion has its own traditions of interpretation.... [There is] no text without interpretation and no interpretation without tradition. Christianity contains a similar principle: 'The letter kills, but the spirit gives life (2 Corinthians 3:6).
>
> Jews, Christians and Muslims have wrestled with the meaning of their scriptures, developing in the process elaborate hermeneutic and jurisprudential systems. (36)

To be sure, we are all subject to the complex impact of the conflicts and difficult standards that are expressed as part of our faith traditions. For example, the declaration of war, how one treats non-believers, and the need to ascertain that one's religious truth is the most, if not only, accurate way to interpret the plan and intentions of God are clearly a most intrinsic part of and definitive of each religious system of belief. However, as Kimball explains in **When Religion Becomes Evil**, and as any student of religious studies knows, one has to be scrupulously careful in remembering that no one person owns the religious truth to the exclusion of others. The *Musar* movement would remind the Jewish community that the strictest of attention to all details must be maintained, including those that may focus on acceptance and proper treatment of those members of the Jewish nation, as well as others, to whom one may not feel a kinship or connection.

By looking at a page of Talmud/*Gemara*, used to explain and distill the many words and ideas of Jewish Law, one learns that so many different people and scholars have such profoundly varied perspectives and comprehensions of the words of God. These discussions are clearly not monolithic but, rather, simultaneously contain passion and hopefully compassion, as well as a few other mandated elements such as humility and respect for others. People change their minds and accept and take on the practices of others after discussion. Other scholars reconsider their initial position and refine it based upon the input of their colleagues. These ongoing dialogues convey the sources that inform and dictate a set of behaviors while simultaneously containing different approaches and adaptations of the indicated standards. Within these important and profound pages of the process of the development of Jewish law and understanding, we must never lose the value of the process of discussion and respectful disagreement itself.

We should not be surprised to learn that this is a known and continuing challenge from the time of our developing Rabbinic tradition. In Pesikta de Rav Kahana 12:25, we read:

> Do not be misled if you hear many voices. Know that I am the One God for each of you.

If we accommodate the fact that we will all hear and discern different ideas as a result of our individuated experience with God, does this take away from the unity that we are to find as believers in God? Would this mean that there is any less compassion (and passion, properly instituted) in one voice that is heard from God as compared to another? Of course, we would then have to confront the challenge of who has the right to determine which understanding is *more appropriate and acceptable,* and of course, more compassionate. Clearly, if this is part of the design of God's words, that we will and perhaps should interpret them in our individuated manner, than who are we to not show compassion for others and their interpretations and understandings regardless of our passion for our own connection to God? This challenge is continually placed before us in our sacred texts. Once again, in the Talmud, in the midst of a discussion found in Shabbat 88b about the words of God and how we hear them, we read as follows:

> This is like a hammer that breaks a rock. Just as this hammer causes the rock to be divided into many slivers, so it is with every single saying and word that went out from the mouth of the Holy One, Blessed Be God, which was divided into seventy languages and interpretations.

One must wonder what our Talmudic teachers understood so very well that has eluded too many of us in our own world and reality. Maybe they knew that it was G-d's compassion that allowed each of us to discern the words of God in a manner that would allow us to have passion for them. So it was compassion (understanding with passion) that led to their passion; today one could make the point that passion takes over and too many do not get back to their own dictated roots of compassion.

At one point in the Torah narrative, Miriam and Aaron complain about their brother Moshe, and how he is treating his wife (***BaMidbar***/Numbers, chapter 12). While the telling of the story is somewhat cryptic and interpreted in various ways as is often the case, one compelling understanding that is shared by many commentators, both contemporary and traditional, is that the siblings claim that God speaks to each of them as well as Moshe and while they are functioning by having relationships and interacting with others, why can't Moshe do the same? They are, in short, concerned about his treatment of his wife, Tzippora; according to this perspective, he is not being the best husband they think he should be in taking care of his wife. God is not pleased with the siblings and explains that Moshe was the most humble of men that God had ever known and that Miriam and Aaron did not totally understand his reality and how he acted. This would be an apt application of the teaching found in Pirke Avot/Ethics of the Fathers, 2: 4,

> Hillel said: Do not separate yourself from the community... Do not judge another until you have been in his place; do not say something that is not readily understood believing that it will be understood (by others).

We learn here that in their passion, Miriam and Aaron did not show compassion in accounting for Moshe's passion. How many times might this be the case in our own lives where we do not have the entire picture and therefore cannot have a complete and comprehensive understanding of how someone else could possibly observe a religious tradition or a given practice in the way that they do, different from our observance and understanding of how we are instructed to act?

This is where the name-calling and the battles between different denominational groupings and religious faith communities take place and escalate to even violent proportions. As we think of the words of Zechariah 14:9, perhaps there is a clue as to how this conflict can be resolved and approached:

> God (HaShem) will be King over the whole world; on that day God will be One and God's name will be One.

We will come together with our different perspectives and voices, as stated by Rav Kahana; and in our acceptance of each other, this is the compassion that we must have and use with passion as we build the world that our religious traditions want us to fashion with each other. This sharing of and commitment to compassion and understanding of each person's passion will reflect the Oneness of God in much the same way as the actions in our daily life reflect the presence of God. It is significant to note that Jews who pray regularly recite this very line at the end of one of the most powerful elements, the *Aleinu*, that is included at the end of our prayer services and gatherings.

It is overwhelming to consider how many times God has cried and regretted what God has created, with the world that was fashioned devoid of this compassion to the degree that God certainly intended and modeled in God's very actions. We return briefly to the beginning of our story of humanity found in the Torah in Bereshit/Genesis 6: 5 – 7, where we have already read as follows:

> God saw the wickedness of Man was great upon the earth, and that every product of the thoughts of his heart was always evil. And God reconsidered having made Man on earth and God had heartfelt sadness. God said, "I will blot out Man whom I created from the face of the earth; from man to animal, to creeping things, and to birds of the sky; for I have reconsidered My having made them.

At this early juncture in the narrative of Torah (Bible or Old Testament), God simultaneously realizes that the very object of God's passion was without compassion. This quality was most important and fundamental to God and it was this quality that was to distinguish the creature that most reflected God's passion. Yet God also understood that the only chance God had for infusing the world with such compassion was through the proper and well guided actions of man, God's established and trusted partner in creation and continuation of the world. Yet, remember that man had to **choose** to act according to such standards. This could not be imposed by God, as difficult as it must have been for God to hold back from doing so. However, given that the special nature of man was to acknowledge the full range of possibilities available to him and then choose in an informed and proper as well as balanced manner, there was no choice, so to speak!

How do we remember this important lesson? We have already established that we are all made, according to Jewish teaching, **BeTzelem Elokim** or in the image of God. Further, we have indicated that there are many ways in which we are to act to reflect this dynamic. What does this actually mean with respect to the components under discussion at this point? We intellectually acknowledge that no two people are exactly alike and that each individual has his or her own potential imprint in our world, including one's sense of passion and compassion. Imagine, for a moment, if we would all intentionally consider that "compassion and humane footprint" with the same attention we might (hopefully) give to our ecological and carbon footprint.

Once again, we look to **Pirke Avot/**Ethics of the Fathers for expression of this ideal and its implications for us as well as our actions with each other in consideration of our attributes of passion and compassion. In 3:18 we learn that

> Akiba would say: Beloved is the human because he was created in the image of God. Greater love was given to this being in that he was created in the image of God as it is said, "In the image of God, God made man."

Clearly the intent is that in the very creation of humanity, compassion was used through the love bestowed upon us. This must be remembered in all of our dealings with each other, as we are motivated simultaneously by passion and compassion in these actions and involvements. Further, as we have already discussed, this motivation as well as the necessary balance we must maintain regarding it is modeled by and found initially with The Creator, our One and Only One God. This is the basis and foundation of **Ethical Monotheism**, the specific Jewish charge given us by the Prophets of Social Justice and at so many other points in the history of our evolving belief in the One and Only One God.

While we work together in this shared mission, we also acknowledge that we each have a special purpose and unique set of goals to accomplish in this world. Just as God has so many different facets and aspects of Being, we are each part of those facets of Being, and must recognize this fact both within ourselves and within others who are part of our collective community of humanity.

In Lubavitch Hassidic tradition, the notion of ***Shlichut*** is a very significant, even foundational principle. The word, itself, means "mission," indicating that we all have a personal mission in this world. Interestingly enough, this word **mission** has a rather powerful meaning in our religious world today, referencing the Jesuit missionaries sent as early as the 1590s. Here mission is about outreaching, that is sending a group to bring religious teaching to others and influence them. Many Hassidic ***Shlichim*** I know make the point that they are not engaged in out-reaching, but rather ***in-reaching***, that is bringing people who want to come and engage in community with them into their spaces. This type of mission is quite different, with the goal of enabling individuals to come to a place of personal fulfillment in their own ways. This is quite different than the notion of ***bringing religion to those on the outside.*** What is so important to remember is that in both of these instances, one being Jewish and one informed by Christian involvement, there is clearly passion and we would hope it is informed properly by compassion.

There is a wonderful story told in Jewish tradition about Reb Zusya. He was always worried about whether or not he was a worthy human being. Was he doing what God wanted him to do, he would perpetually and constantly ask of himself. Was he wealthy enough? Was he successful enough? Had he been a good leader? Was he compassionate and humble enough? Did he use the resources he had been given in proper and intended manners? He mused that once he would leave this world, God would ask him if he had been as good as Moses, or David or Solomon or Jacob or any number of known and well regarded Jewish sages and teachers in terms of these qualities. Reb Zusya lived his life and then left this world. As he met God, he was asked, "So Zusya, were you the best Zusya you could possibly have been? Were you a compassionate and caring being to the best of your ability?

Therefore, as we continue in the stories and lore of our Jewish traditions and literature, we watch succeeding generations of people learn how to be compassionate, how to feel for and empathize with others, all of whom are also created by God. This is what is at the heart of, many would claim, the most powerful motivating factor of Creation. It is this compassion that remains at one and the same time our greatest gift and our most formidable challenge. This is truly the manner in which we are to emulate Our Creator through the actions of our lives, living in the image of God.

Without this religion fails, while if we can successfully incorporate it in our lives, religion as an institution has incredible potential to continue to help us in our own desire and hope to heal and improve our world and our human family with our humanity.

Questions for Continued Thought and Discussion:

1. What evokes the feeling of passion in you the most? About what and/or whom do you feel most passionate?

2. What evokes the feeling of compassion in you the most? About what and/or whom do you feel most compassionate?

3. What elements of compassion do you think all people of faith can potentially share?

4. What is dangerous about passion if it is not properly tempered; how do we remember and learn to do so?

5. What could be *your **Shlichut*** in the world to which you can contribute so much based upon both your passion and compassion?

IX. A Few Important and Timeless Teachers

Make for yourself a teacher, acquire for yourself a friend, and judge every person favorably and give him the benefit of the doubt.

Pirke Avot, 1:6

Once again as we search the Teachings of our Fathers, we find sage advice as we try to insure that we live meaningful and purposeful lives. We are familiar with the phase "no man is an island" and here this is reinforced as we are adjoined to connect in meaningful ways to appropriate colleagues and mentors. Further, the last part of this quoted instruction provides additional direction in making such important and valuable choices as we surround ourselves with others with and from whom we can learn in our journey through life, remembering that many different teachers and friends can and do enrich our lives in so many different ways, if we are open to such explorations.

As we survey history and the many generations that preceded us, we certainly are aware of the many teachers and exemplars that have bestowed upon us such important lessons through the instruction of their lives and the example of their deeds. This is the legacy they leave for us to continue and our challenge is to add our own imprint to this collective experience. In this way, we continue the generational transmission discussed earlier, the extension of the values and experiences of our lives from one generation to the next one – ***midor ledor***. Certainly this is the intent of the Native Americans in their understanding of generational transmission through shared actions between those generations and the various individuals who so instruct as opposed to passing on of the written word, the continuation of the legacy we all craft through the example, experience and actions of our lives.

Think of the importance and value of mentoring relationships in our lives today in so many different venues, whether for professional purposes, goals of character development, involvement in support groups as discussed earlier, or otherwise. Through structured sharing and mutual efforts, we learn and teach by example, hopefully enhancing each other with compassion in sharing our passion and so much else. As another example of such sharing and investment of human beings in each other, consider successful and meaningful parent/child relationships and those between teachers and students as well. How many times have we quoted a favorite teacher or applied the wisdom and lessons of experience of older relatives in our own lives?

Each one of us should consider who those teachers and exemplars are for us in our own lives as well as the lessons and legacy they leave us which we wish to continue in our own journeys and involvements. In engaging in this exercise, we must consider what our own foundational values and principles are, in terms of thinking about those teachers and mentors that characterize these important standards of behavior and being in our lives. There are no limits here; we can claim as many teachers, exemplars, and friends as we wish. They can be well known to the masses or beloved personally by us individually. To help jump-start this process, allow me to present some of my own favorite teachers and the lessons they have bestowed upon me and my life, which I, in turn, try, intend and hope to be privileged to impart to all those with whom I come in contact.

As should clearly be apparent to the reader by this point, life has never appeared as simple or less than complex and multi-dimensional for me. I understand the many different sides of the coin (many more than two, incidentally, when accounting for the facets of the rim) and that as we are each crafted as unique and singular individuals, so too are the ideas and composite personality we each bring to the collective table we will call community. This community extends indefinitely across the miles of our globe and the generations of our history. Our favorite and most meaningful teachers can be from any point, either vertically or horizontally, in that larger community of humanity, truly the most extensive ***chat room*** imaginable before technology taught us what that concept is and can be in our lives.

The first teacher I choose to discuss is Job, as well as his three (or four, depending on who you count) different friends, with their personal set of goals and individuated approaches to Job and his dilemma. Job, as you will recall, was the person who had it all and whose story is told in the Jewish Bible. He had health, family, wealth, and position in community --- apparently the ideal life, as we know it! He was also incredibly and unwaveringly faithful to God. In fact, as we read in the very beginning of this narrative:

> There was a man in the land of Uz named Job. That man was blameless and upright: he feared God and shunned evil. (1:1)

Job would continually thank and worship God without fail. As a response to this unyielding faith, God was challenged by God's adversary, (the) ***satan***, a curious, complex, and quite troublesome figure in Jewish texts and tradition. The challenge levied at God by this member of the Heavenly Beings was the claim that this absolute devotion on the part of this man from Uz could very well be and most likely was because Job had everything, so why would he not acknowledge and pray to God. ***Satan*** then proceeds to propose to God that if everything were to be taken away from Job, perhaps then he would not be so faithful and unwavering. God responds to the challenge by informing ***Satan*** that he may do what he wishes to Job, but only his person he may not touch.

At this point, we watch as all those things that caused Job to feel so duly blessed are removed from him, one by one in painful succession. In the meantime each of his friends – Eliphaz, Bildad and Zophar, as well as Elihu at a later point – engage in theological and philosophical dialogue with him about his situation, his questions and faith, and the ramifications of his life journey as it evolves. As one watches Job and monitors the extent of his angst, it is difficult not to imagine and have some reaction to his pain.

By Chapter Ten of this narrative, we read as follows (10: 1 – 7):

> I am disgusted with my life;
> I will give in to my complaint,
> Speaking in the bitterness of my soul.
> I tell God, "Do not condemn me;
> Let me know what you charge me with.
> Does it benefit You to defraud your work;
> To despise the toil of Your hands;
> While smiling on the advice of the wicked?
> Do You have the eyes of flesh?
> Is Your vision that of mere men?
> Are Your days the days of a mortal?
> Are Your years the years of a human?
> Why are you seeking my iniquity
> And trying to find my sin?
> You know that I am not guilty,
> And that no one will deliver me from Your hand."

Job clearly has become a universal figure in the complexity and conflict of remaining faithful in the midst of horrible and tragic suffering. So many theologians, philosophers, and adherents within many faith communities explore his experience as they try to find answers and come to terms with their own life and challenges to faith and belief. In fact, included in some of these commentaries and explorations of this text is a most important challenge, namely who exactly is on trial in this troubling narrative, Job or G-d! In the text quoted here, the case could be made for the latter. Alternatively, perhaps Job is the case study to test his friends, or to consider yet another possibility, maybe it is us who is put on trial by the incredulous situation – namely, could any of us remain faithful in such dire circumstances?

One approach to consider comes to us from Zophar who reminds Job that while man might respond to such reasonable logic and feel compelled to provide a well-constructed answer, he certainly cannot expect God to present as a respondent directly in such a discourse. This need is reflective of the nature of man and the inherent limitations of being human, not God and God's extensive range of understanding. God's mysteries and the secrets of God's wisdom are simply not within the purview of the human (Job, Chapter 11). Once again, the point made earlier about limitations and boundaries that exist in the God-man relationship are confirmed. We have questions and challenges for God, but given that we operate in different spheres, the reality is that the people whom G-d has created and who continue to believe in God's ways will not come to a complete and comprehensive understanding of God and God's ways. In fact, this is inherently impossible for only God can comprehend God in this realm of theological thinking. However, the fact that we still consider these questions that are relentless in confronting and challenging our very being is what is supremely significant. These questions and the valuing of the search that they represent have also been passed from generation to generation as much as any traditions and declarative teachings.

Through the personalities of the friends of Job and their dialogue we learn that questioning is such an important part of our faith and our very being, another point confirmed consistently through these essays and texts. Additionally, we know that in our questioning, we will arrive at varied points, taking different approaches and discerning different answers. Martin Buber taught us an important aspect of this intellectual and human reality when he said that "Questions unite, answers divide." How wonderful it is to share our questions, our yearning and the realization that we may not be "quite sure" about how aspects of our life turn out.

This is certainly a most important lesson of the book of Job. In the end of this narrative, Job gets the ultimate "do over" with new children, new wealth, a new position and so forth. It must be pointed out, however, that in the various artistic and literary renditions and adaptations of this universal story, this is not always the case. In one case, a Canadian playwright named Jason Sherman produced a stage play based on the story of Job in 1998 called **Patience**. In the play, true to its template and original inspiration, Reuben, who is Sherman's Job, once had it all and lost everything. The last scene ends as its main protagonist walks off stage alone with nothing but the hope of a possible new beginning of which even he is not certain, and both despondent and perhaps resigned to the notion that we are random specks of dust wandering around in a vast universe, just biding our time until death (37). In yet another retelling, JB: A Play in Verse by Archibald MacLeish, Job and his wife agree to hold onto each other and their hope for something better as they look at their broken life together (38). As the various curtains close on these versions of the Biblical narrative of the tragic Job and others that have also been penned, we are left with our own ultimate questions as we consider the many different options placed before us. How do we handle our good fortune? What do we do when our suffering replaces blessings? To what degree do we hold God responsible? What part do we, and our own actions play in such downturns? Is there always a cause; or can it be random and what are the implications of the latter possibility?

Here is validation of the notion that we can each approach God individually and differently. As we have seen, this permission for the multi-vocality of our responses to God runs through Jewish texts and teachings as a strong and consistent thread. Consider for example the following text from the beginning of the ***Amidah***, the core prayer unit that Jews who pray daily may repeat at least three times, with additional readings and renditions on Shabbat and special days of observance.

> Blessed by You God Our Lord, King of the world, God of our fathers, God of Abraham, God of Isaac, and God of Jacob…

In some of our Jewish prayer communities, our Matriarchs are also added to the list. In these instances, the reading of this first part of the prayer is as follows:

> Blessed be You God Our Lord, King of the world, God of our fathers, God of Abraham, God of Isaac, and God of Jacob, God of Sarah, God of Rebecca, God of Leah and God of Rachel …

Count the number of times that the words "God of" is used in this one part of the first sentence of this important and core element of Jewish liturgy. Why do you think that this text does not just read much more simply as follows – "God of our fathers and our mothers, Abraham, Isaac…?" I would suggest that this wording aptly represents the truism that we each have individuated and specific experiences of God and the reason that this listing appears as it does acknowledges that one person's experience of God may and most likely will be wholly different than that experienced by another. Likewise, the big questions and challenges that we confront in life will evoke different answers and lead to various approaches for different people. This is a most valuable lesson we learn from all of our Matriarchs, Patriarchs, Prophets, Talmudic teachers, and so many others through the pages of our history and the texts that chronicle its events and ideas. We see this lesson as well with Job and his friends, JB and those in his life and Reuben and his colleagues and family; how do we extrapolate and apply this lesson to our own lives? This question is the most important lesson I learn from the narrative of Job.

Elisha ben Abuyah, a *Tanna* or teacher in the beginning of the second century of the Common Era, is yet another figure who is remembered for his pain and tragic ending and there is so much that we can learn from his experience and angst. While he also evokes anger and disdain in many corners of the Jewish community of religious adherents for losing his faith and connection to the Jewish community in the end, it is important to consider that all might not have been as lost and simple as it seemed when looking carefully at what we know about his story. Here is a wonderful example of where we apply the dictum of not judging another until we are standing in his or her place. The tragedy of Elisha is that he is torn between the two vastly different worlds into which he was born, the Greek world to which his father (Abuyah) was drawn and the Jewish world of his mother's family. Elisha ben Abuyah was most drastically torn between the logic found, or not found, in the reason of the secular world and the logic found, or not found, in the faith of the religious world.

It might appear that any attempts to reconcile the two were foiled apparently in one of the most well-known explanations in the Talmud (***Kiddushin*** 39b) when Elisha watched a young boy show respect for his father (observing the ***Mitzvah*** of ***Kibbud Av v'Em*** – honoring your father and mother) by listening to his father and climbing a ladder to send a mother bird away from the nest before taking eggs (known as ***Shiluach Kan***) and then falling from the ladder on which he was standing and die. The reward indicated in the Torah is the same for observance of each of these ***Mitzvot***, namely that the boy should live a long life and he should have a good and fulfilling life – and here, he dies instantly in his youth!

168

This sequence of events made no sense to Elisha's understanding of life and priorities and we are told that perhaps it was this seemingly senseless loss of young life that caused him to ultimately give up on the conflict he confronted and turn away from Judaism at the end.

Additionally there were other horrors that he witnessed, which is highly likely given the timing of his life during the Bar Kochba revolt and the persecutions that followed. Not being able to reconcile the absolutely inhumane things he witnessed, he asked what reward could possibly come from Torah; certainly not what he observed based on what he had learned! Further, he is one of the four Rabbis who tradition tells us came to the gates of Paradise, engaged in the secrets of intense study, and the one who turned away and rejected all that he had learned, becoming a heretic. Additionally there are stories of his absolute turning away from Jewish life and practice in a variety of sources, as well as disdain for and even possible participation in persecution of the Jewish community.

It is important for us not to get lost in the criticism of Elisha ben Abuyah and to remember the circumstances of his life. In parallel accounts in the Jerusalem Talmud (***Talmud Yerushalmi***) and the Babylonian Talmud (***Talmud Bavli***) in ***Masechet Hagiga*** (77b and 15 a – b respectively), we see the expression of the pain and dejection that becomes Elisha's destiny, while Rabbi Meir, his prized student maintains the teachings that Elisha had imparted to him and tries to use them to bring his beloved teacher back to his roots and his faith in God. It is interesting, chilling even, to note that in their conversation, the text and life of none other than Job is evoked when Meir states that Job is rewarded at the end of his life by being given so much more. Elisha rejects this reasoning, stating that for those who have died and been taken from this earth there is no sense of reward. It appears that he was reflecting on his own life and reactions to an excessive amount of tragedy witnessed during it.

While his many students and teachers are not named and ultimately abandoned him, this most celebrated pupil, Rabbi Meir, remained connected to him until the end. Supposedly, it is through this student that teachings and the scholarship of Elisha ben Abuyah were continued as part of the generational transmission process within the Jewish learning community. So while Elisha ben Abuyah may have been lost to the Jewish community, his teachings, the most intimate part of his soul, remained and continued to influence and inspire. Further, one should consider that perhaps some of the brilliance and depth of his scholarship and teachings may very well have come from and be attributed to the very conflict between his two worlds that plagued him through his life. While those who feel abandoned by Elisha ben Abuyah refer to him as The Other/***Acher***, others may very well feel the pain and irony of life that he articulated through his actions and angst.

Again, as with Job, we have a universal story here that invites renditions and retellings of his life as so many try to come to terms with this difficult narrative of such a celebrated scholar as Elisha ben Abuyah and his bitter end. Probably the most well-known is Milton Steinberg's As a Driven Leaf (United States of America: Behrman House, 1939). The irony and profound meaning of the popularity of these two figures in later literature and study cannot go unnoticed. We obviously want to know what happens to faith with the most knowledgeable and most dedicated to God when tragedy strikes. How do we as limited humans hold onto our center of faith in God when our lives implode? This to me is a most important legacy that Elisha ben Abuyah leaves us. The same appears to be true for the next chosen teacher.

Kohelet or Ecclesiastes, whom many believe to have been King Solomon (or alternatively, someone of that station in life), and whom we have already mentioned regarding his understanding of wisdom among other reasons, may appear to be the antithesis of Elisha ben Abuyah and Job in that his life was and appeared to remain privileged and successful by any measure. Conflicts in this life were between offerings and their value, not so much completely and exclusively different contexts for living that life. His task was to try to figure out what it was that he was supposed to do and which of several options to pursue in terms of living a meaningful life. Further, as many take this book to be authored later in the life of King Solomon, at a point when the vast experiences and opportunities that he would have had would place him in a singularly unique position to judge between these various options in terms of their ultimate worth. Yet here too, he finds the very reality and presence of this choice to be vexing and filled with angst that was often too much to bear. While one could make the point that this conflict was of a more intellectualized nature, does this make it any less significant in terms of existential crises?

He acknowledges in the ongoing refrain of **there is nothing new under the sun** that we will, through the generations that come and go, transmit this angst and while this is new and unique for each thoughtful and able person who considers it, there is nothing new about the struggle itself. It is as natural as the wind that blows and its appearance in our lives will be an ever-present constant.

In Chapter One, verses four through eleven, part of which was briefly cited earlier, we read that

> One generation goes and another generation comes; and the earth continues forever. The sun rises and the sun goes down; and hurries to take the place where it rose. The wind blows southward and turns northward turning around and around, and on its rounds the wind always returns ... All of these things are tiring, no man can ever speak of them, the eye never sees enough of them, and the ear is not fulfilled

from hearing it. Whatever happened before, this is what will happen and what has already occurred, this is what will occur; there is nothing new beneath the sun. Sometimes there is a thing for which it is said, 'look this is new,' but actually this already occurred many times before. Earlier occurrences are not remembered; and neither are the ones that come later to be any more remembered than those that will occur at the very end.

The notion of repetition and familiarity in our lives and in the world in which we live might seem to bring comfort. However, for Kohelet, it is the source of his frustration, that no matter how privileged a person is and what they accomplish and what they have, in the end we all meet the same destiny that the mortality that is a fact of our lives brings with it. He questions the very value and purpose of life and any joy that it might bring in light of this truth about the end of all human beings.

One articulation of this precise dilemma is found in Chapter Two when he is trying to discern whether or not there is any advantage to the wise person for not being a fool. In Chapter Two, verses fourteen through sixteen, he muses as follows:

> A wise man has his eyes in his head and the fool walks in darkness, and I also observed that the same fate awaits them both. So I said in my heart, if the fate of the fool will also be my fate, then what advantage do I have by being wise? I said in my heart that this too is futile. Because there is no memory of the wise man or the fool forever and as the days roll by, everyone is forgotten and the wise man dies just like the fool.

This tone is continued throughout this thought journal that many find to be painfully sad. In fact, one of the most compelling explanations regarding when we read this book in our synagogues, which is on

Sukkot, also called ***Zeman Simchateinu*** or "time of our joy," is that only at such a supremely happy time could we read such a depressing piece as ***Kohelet***. Alternatively, I often challenge people by asking them to consider whether they see this book as one of resignation, affirmation or reconciliation. Is the statement of the truths that ***Kohelet*** has come to observe possibly an indication of the understanding that ultimately those who pose such questions will realistically reach? Does this understanding help us or bring us more pain?

As we accompany ***Kohelet*** on his journey through what he sees as the various choices that life presents – eat, drink and be merry ***or*** gather wisdom to the degree that you can – we are challenged to look at the bigger picture. What is the legacy that we in fact leave for others when we have finished our earthly tasks? One is forced to take note that obviously the writer of this text has achieved a type of immortality as these words and teachings are still passed from generation to generation today, so many generations and worlds after they were composed. To be sure, as one generation comes and another goes and the world remains and continues forever, so does the collection of teachings and traditions of all those who have gone before us. We continue their lives and their legacies in a very real way by using and keeping alive the teachings and wisdom they have left for us. Perhaps in some way, within the wisdom of ***Kohelet***, this was known, and therein lies the most poignant lesson of all. Namely, that whether resulting from tragedy of unfathomable loss as in the case of Job; or through a complete loss of faith in all that matters as is the lot of Elisha ben Abuyah; or as a by-product of "knowing and experiencing too much" as may have been the case with Solomon; in the end, we are all confronted with the same human limitations that plague us all and there are simply questions we will never be able to answer, though we will never stop asking them.

Today, there seems to be a plethora of academic scholars, theologians, artists and so many creative and intelligent individuals asking these very questions and engaging us in the same dialogue as we all try to uncover the ultimate secrets and underlying reasons for our existence. These searching souls are using religion as much as art, drama, as often as mathematics, science, song and philosophical journeys, and virtually every imaginable field of endeavor as a venue for this treasure hunt as we seek the *ultimate* answers, or better yet, approaches to the *big* questions that continue to confront us. As we all search for these answers, we continue to affirm the notion that the journey is more important than reaching the ultimate goal, which by its very nature, will continue to elude us. When we come to realization of this point, we share both the wisdom and angst of **Kohelet.**

There are many other teachers from our past that we could easily include at this point. Rather, lets shift the focus to how we can learn so many important and vital lessons from each other in our daily lives. There are seemingly occasional contacts we each have either directly or by the most removed of associations with the teacher in all of us. If we are aware of their existence and pay close attention, we can discern many lessons from the people and interactions in our lives every day.

Years ago, I was watching a segment of Oprah Winfrey on which she was explaining that she had a recurring dream in which she was flying a bit above the earth's surface and met many children along the way. She explained that when she would go by a child, she would ask that child, "How are you?" The reply that she continued to receive from every child she passed by was "That is not the right question to ask. You should ask me what were you sent to teach me today?" What a wonderful question for all of us! We should constantly be considering what we were sent here to teach each other and learn from and with each other. This is our mission, that ***Shlichut***, about which the Lubavitch teach us.

Sometimes these are huge lessons and sometimes, they will be seemingly small lessons in opportune moments, which in retrospect can be the largest ones of all. Years ago (decades, actually), when in my childhood years I was attending Hebrew School in Baltimore, Maryland, I had a teacher by the name of Helen B. Shefferman. She has since died (may her memory be for a blessing, ***Zichrona LeShalom***), but she lives on every day I have contact with students, colleagues and the various people with whom I interact in a most important manner. She taught me to care about and watch everyone very carefully, both in words and deeds. How did she do this?

On Thanksgiving morning, when I was ten years old, the phone rang in my home. I answered the phone and it was Mrs. Shefferman wanting to speak with my parents. I, of course, was petrified trying to imagine what horrible thing I had done that warranted such a call. This was particularly upsetting since I was always the "perfect little student," attentive and conscientious in all that I did. So what was the problem and why was this teacher calling *my parents*? It turned out that this lovely and caring lady had called my parents to ask what she could do to help me since I did not seem to be happy in her class. I was absolutely floored that my teacher would take time out of her well-earned vacation days to call my parents to find out what was wrong because it seemed that I was not happy.

Until today, I make such calls and overtures to students and parents. Every time I do so, the lessons Mrs. Shefferman taught me are reenacted and part of her is kept alive and passed on to other members of our larger community of humanity. I always "watch eyeballs" ever so carefully ***B'zechut Helen Shefferman z'l***, in the memory of Helen Shefferman, may her memory be for a blessing.

Her legacy continues to provide instruction and guidance for us all in caring about each other in a genuine manner.

These lessons are indeed everywhere and can be applied anywhere, yet another attainment of immortality for those from whom we learn and in whose merit we act and remember. Another one of my teachers, this one during my high school years, was Dr. Louis Kaplan, also of blessed memory – ***Zichrono LeShalom***. One of the most important parts of my life is my work to build bridges of understanding between disparate groups within the Jewish community, attempting to achieve a sense of unity or ***Achdut***, another foundational Jewish aspiration. In different venues, I also try to achieve bridges of understanding among different faith communities and other groups of different or conflicting identity. This is, I feel, an important and fundamental part of my own mission or ***Shlichut*** in this world. As I often state, there are enough people who are judgmental; my role is to be accepting while not compromising my own standards of ritual as well as behavior.

I attribute the beginning of this work in my life to Dr. Kaplan. I remember him well as I remember my conversations and interactions about the ***big*** questions of life, religion and philosophy in which we were engaged during those critically important formative years in my life. I knew that Dr. Kaplan was about as left to the spectrum of Jewish thinking and processing of Halacha as one could be in so many ways (in fact many of us from Baltimore think of him as just another "Reconstructionist Kaplan") and he must have had more than a few disagreements with some of the ideas I set forth, being rather traditional and Halachically oriented in my thinking. Nonetheless, I never felt judged, threatened or exposed to anything less than respect and regard for what I believed, that is, for my foundational truths. Through graciously sharing his attentive ear, years of knowledge and wisdom, and probing questions, Dr. Kaplan taught me that we can (and must!) discuss, learn, and explore together while we agree to disagree about some aspects of what we are sharing, no matter how fundamental those disagreements may be. He never explained this to me; he just did it! This too, I try to convey through my actions and involvements in all aspects of my life. Dr. Kaplan continues to teach from the school in the heavens, or as it is called, the **Yeshivah LeMa'aleh**, through these efforts of this humble eternal student.

A final most compelling example is the most important lesson I learned many years ago about priorities from Golda Meir who was Prime Minister of Israel. There was always a strong maternal presence about her and she was often referred to as the "Mother" of her country of Israel. She in turn remarked from time to time about how ironic it was that she was much more the mother of a country than she could have been to and for her children. This had to be a most difficult admission on her part and made an indelible impression on me as I found myself in the position of making various choices and plans as the trajectory of my own professional life evolved.

I have been fortunate and blessed enough to have an amazing professional career and life, and pray that it will continue to be a successful and meaningful experience in the years to come. Within the context of this blessed life, I am a wife to my incredible husband and mother to four amazing children as well as actively involved in the families that they are building, all truly gifts from God. Every choice I have made is with these most important people in my life in mind. If I have made a professional decision or not accepted an impressive offer that might seem to be ill informed in terms of exposure and professional mobility, it was always a choice and ***not*** a sacrifice. I have always been acutely aware that if I had made a choice that was good professionally but not good for my family, whom I love and cherish dearly, ***that*** would have been a sacrifice – one I would have profoundly regretted no matter how far life would have taken me. What better lesson can one learn from another and what better legacy can one leave for another? Thank you, ***Todah Rabbah***, to all of these amazing valued teachers and so many more.

Questions for Continued Thought and Discussion:

1. Who are some of your most amazing teachers and what have they taught you?

2. How did these amazing teachers impart their lessons to you?

3. How have these lessons contributed to your life in significant ways personally and professionally?

4. What are the most important lessons you hope to impart to those with whom you come in contact?

5. What legacy of lessons do you hope to leave as an imprint on this world?

X. Soft Souls in a Rough World

Let us make the people in our image, after our likeness...
And God created man in God's image,
In the image of God they were created

Refrain from Bereshit/Genesis 1: 26 - 27

I love the relatively simple but infinitely profound expression, "God don't make junk." Jewish thinking and philosophy teaches us to see the good in people and to try to access it in any way we can. Christianity teaches forgiveness and both religions teach, as do many others, to love and consider your friend or neighbor as you would yourself, and to work on behalf of those around us. Islam teaches submission to God's will and acting accordingly in all aspects of one's life. How many of us take these basic and foundational principles of our respective communities and the teachings that guide them seriously and judge ourselves by this benchmark, while we are so engrossed in many of the ritual aspects of our individual lives?

I have often commented to my children, "I am not intolerant of anything except intolerance." At this point, they gently and correctly have reminded me that this too is intolerance. Yes, this may seem difficult to comprehend but it is a fair challenge if you stop to think earnestly about it. How do we continue to 'give others the benefit of the doubt' according to Jewish teachings and 'turn the other cheek' as our Christian friends remind us? How many chances do we give another who has habitually hurt us, and how do we reconcile the clear and abhorrent injustices of our world with our senses and sensibilities? How do we have sympathy for and 'tolerate' minimally as well as love and cherish maximally the other who is not tolerant of us?

During the past years and decades, there have been ongoing reports of Israeli doctors who have treated Palestinians, including those who are injured during their intentional infliction of harm on Israeli citizens. Some time ago, there was an incident of an Israeli doctor working to save the life of a Palestinian suicide bomber, with wounds that resulted during a bombing he initiated. This doctor was observing his ethical, personal, professional and Jewish codes of honor seriously in working to save the life of this human being entrusted to his care.

After completion of the life-saving procedures that were needed, the patient remarked emphatically that he would go right out to the streets and do what he did before, continuing to attempt killing as many Israelis and Jews as possible as soon as he recovered from his injuries. So many of us in various communities were horrified by this statement, and yet it is part of our reality. We may too often find ourselves in circumstances where we use our values to save lives that do not value us, or our lives. Based on those values, we treat others with far more concern and care then they will ever send our way. However inequitable this may seem, it is precisely in these unfair equations, that our true sense and application of values and intrinsic teachings are tested.

Regardless of this patient's reaction, the doctor acted honorably and properly, and were he to have the opportunity to rethink his position, given this reaction, he would have had to act in the same way again. This was his responsibility as a Jew, as a physician and as an honorable human being.

It is supremely difficult for those of us who take the needs and fragility of humanity seriously and work in a variety of ways to better our world, once again enacting the Jewish concept of ***Tikkun Olam***, to work alongside and constructively with those who do not.

I often say that the only thing I can do with my standards and ideals is to live by them, raise my children with them and then try to interact with others using them. I cannot impose them on another. Not all would agree with me and many do feel that their way is the only right way, no matter what!

In the Jewish world, we are taught that community building and sharing of values are inextricably tied together. Yet we have to once again be mindful of a tricky balance, in this case that of responsibility of the group for each other juxtaposed with the understanding that we cannot be oppressive in exercising this responsibility. Our sages remind us that

> All of Israel is responsible, one for the other/ ***Kol Yisrael arevim zeh b'zeh.***

An Israeli friend and colleague once explained to my husband that his understanding of this idea was that we are commanded to love each other ***so much*** that we have to implore, teach and work until we reach and successfully convince each other what we know to be right, no matter what extreme measures have to be used to do so. While this is understandable on one level, it also leads to obviously problematic and destructive excesses in the reality that confronts us daily as explored elsewhere in these essays.

Years ago, I was at a professional conference to which I took my family for almost thirty years as a type of pilgrimage. It was one of my absolute favorite weeks of the year, for at this conference Jews of all denominational groupings, professional pursuits, and individual personalities came together for a week of Jewish living and learning together. It would not be an understatement to say that this community was the closest to my concept or ideal of Utopia in my experience and the practicality of my life. Even in this setting, not all understood, there were those who could not accept others, and problems ensued bringing disappointment that could be sometimes rather profound, given the expectations many brought to this ingathering of so many different Jewish educators and their families.

One Shabbat at this annual community gathering, our oldest daughter came to find me because a friend of hers was very upset even in this collective of such special people. A group of teenagers were playing basketball at a specified place on the campus and as people were walking about and resting during the afternoon, some of the more "strictly observant Jewish" individuals that were members of this larger pluralistic community became angry and chided the teenagers for not wearing "modest and appropriate clothing" on Shabbat (they were wearing sports and casual clothing, not skimpy bathing suits or spandex). My daughter's friend was extremely upset and bewildered, as she did not think that she and her friends were doing anything wrong. Her comment to me was "I thought everyone here accepted everyone else. I thought that we could all come together here with our differences. I thought this was an ideal place." We then sat and spoke, as I explained that this special place was indeed ideal; what it was not was idyllic.

What was in fact ideal about this space and community that defined it was that generally there was acceptance and understanding among the many different groups found in this setting. However, it was important to note that this was *generally* the case, not necessarily manifested by all individuals at all moments. That would indeed be *idyllic*. What was also *ideal* was that when the realities of the outside world crept in and when one Jew would judge or somehow invalidate another in any way, there was a great deal of support to help each other address such challenges and upset. There will always be those who do not accept us, do not agree with what we do, and feel that they must judge us. Sometimes, this may feel like, as my Israeli friend put it, we love each other so much we have to implore, teach and work until we successfully force each other to understand what we know to be right. However, just as the proverbial excess of the mother who smothers with her love, we must take care to watch those around us carefully and hold ourselves accountable for the impact of our actions on each other, on the other members of our community and our families.

At this point in our evolution as a world community and with respect to the hold that ***fundamentalism*** and its effects have on us as individuals and community members, it is supremely important to consider the balance of the vigilance of our intentions and the impact of our actions. Those of us who are aware of maintaining the integrity of this balance in our lives watch our words carefully, try to anticipate what others need and walk very carefully through the obstacle course we call life. In doing so, we are following the teaching of ***Pirke Avot*** 1:10, in which we learn to "judge the other person favorably and give them the benefit of the doubt." Obviously not all people do this. Those of us who do live by such standards meet with frustration too often in spite of our own Herculean efforts to accept others and build a constructive and cooperative community of acceptance.

Once again, we can hear and feel The Creator of all beings, God, cry at our collective failure in not meeting the standard of caring for and about the feelings of each other and genuinely being attuned to the effect of our own actions. The parent who lives in such a manner might look at their children daily and wonder if they are doing them any favor. Should we not teach our children to have a thick skin, to defend themselves proactively against the injustices and wrongs of the world, putting themselves first? Could we not make the case that any parent who does not do just that is not fulfilling their responsibility to their children? Many would state just that position!

However, just as Robert Bly would have us work to influence the next generation and as we have seen this dynamic of generational transmission as critical to our society, those amongst us who have "soft souls" must take great care not to lose them to the harsh realities and damage caused by the rough winds of our experience and life. How do we pass that on to our children while equipping them for survival in the realities of our world? Soft souls have a responsibility to maintain a presence in our world and help to enable and encourage other soft souls. If reality crept into the ideal of the special community described above, then we must consider how we allow our ideals to gallop into our reality and hopefully influence it in a most positive and constructive manner.

This was Harold Rugg's idea of ***Social Reconstructionism*** as espoused in the 1930's, namely that there are institutions (in his case, schools) that should reflect society and the surrounding community at its best. However, he explained, when society is not at its best, these institutions should reflect the hopes for the best and ultimately incite its sponsoring society or community to come closer to its own set of ideals, and be better if not best. In other words, Rugg would have us consider schools as laboratories for societal change and improvement (39). Many would agree that this is a most noble goal for our educational institutions to attain. Ultimately, the individuals that are produced and refined by their experiences in these laboratories will determine the degree to which this objective is achieved, and how they apply their well-learned lessons in various pursuits as we work together to improve our world and reality.

Interestingly enough, the work of Rugg is not universally known and those who have studied his work and philosophy note that he was a man before his time; perhaps his time has arrived. Are we ready to hold ourselves to the degree of accountability that Rugg would place before us; will we ever be ready for such self-examination and discipline in working for the collective good of the whole in a meaningful and dedicated manner, beginning with our schools and the youth we entrust to their training, and fanning out to the whole of our society in reaching our ideal?

It is so interesting and enlightening to watch young children for whom much of this is often, though certainly not always, so easy. They accept each other in a simple way that often eludes us as we grow and mature. With the right environment, this natural inclination can be nurtured and further developed so that they will continue to care for and be invested in each other. Unfortunately, what actually happens as they grow and develop is the opposite as small children who played together will grow up and have nothing to do with each other due to learned behaviors and standards of the surrounding society. The familiar message of "you have to be carefully taught to hate" from *South Pacific* seems to continue as a refrain in our lives today. It is encouraging and important to note, however, that there are an increasing number of programs and efforts in place to try to turn this tide and have these children continue to feel invested in each other as they grow. While this is clearly due to the necessity of the nature of our reality, nonetheless, it can give us a reason to feel somewhat hopeful.

In our contemporary communities of diversity, children of different faiths, ethnic groupings, races and other identity points are encouraged to appreciate their differences and build a community of caring and cooperation. Our own family is indeed fortunate to live in such a committed community of diversity and we have found that as our children have gone on to University and choosing communities in which to live, this is something they intentionally seek, as we did years ago. In Israel, there are efforts to work with Israeli and Palestinian Arab children and families to live together, learn together, and develop meaningful relationships with each other. The *Yad b'Yad* bi-lingual school system, programs at *Givat Haviva*, Teachers' colleges, Universities, basketball teams, circus troupes and so many other entities bring Israelis, Arabs, Jews, Muslims,

Palestinians and others of all ages together for shared experiences. In the United States, many efforts and independent initiatives are similarly dedicated to creating meaningful bridges of understanding and acceptance across lines of nationality, cultural background, religion, ethnicity, race and so many other points of identity. There are many noble attempts to create communities that subscribe to the ideal of loving the other as one loves oneself in a positive and constructive way. The potential contribution that participants in these programs can make to the world at large is clearly boundless. One would certainly hope that Harold Rugg would be proud as well as comforted to know that his message was not lost with the passage of generations and time, and that his legacy as a teacher has been preserved as well.

Yet, too often, even the successful graduates of such programs too quickly devolve and resort to the least common denominator of tolerance or acceptance in their relationships with others once they are exposed to the rough winds of the real world. We can create as many of these "laboratories" as we want; the question and challenge is how to insure that those who benefit from such programs really do change the world in a meaningful and constructive manner once they exit these comparatively enclosed cocoons. For a variety of reasons, one of our four children was educated primarily in our public school district which is a registered No Place for Hate © school system and as a young adult in his college years has discovered how challenging it can indeed be in finding a community that is as embracing and respectful of differences and committed to inclusion of all community members as was our school district. In sharing his story with others, I find other parents who live in our community, whose children are experiencing the same problems.

How do those who have experienced the support and validation of such a group wade through the obstacle course of real life when that support and validation are no longer there to support the set of values and standards they hold to be true? How does such a person hold on to their ideals and principles and not be compromised by the discord of the larger world in which they may not so easily find these ideals to be present? Here we are once again reminded of the power and the importance of community in Jewish teachings. This is precisely why Abraham had to cease his efforts to convince God to save the people of Sodom and Gomorrah, for he could not find the minimum of ten people who were righteous; and without this small critical mass, individuals would not be able to achieve what needed to be done on a community wide basis.

I always find the Jewish maxim of ***know before Whom you stand*** to be a powerful reminder of both our humanity and The Creator to whom we are all ultimately responsible. We all stand before God according to the source of this statement, and are simultaneously always accountable to ourselves as well as each other. Some, if not most, of us have heard and probably know the teaching ***to thine own self be true,*** which certainly could be thought to express a similar sentiment. For the soft souls amongst us, this could be and probably is part of our mission, our ***Shlichut***, in this world.

Once again, we find support for such an approach in our Jewish sources. We have already seen that we are to model the behaviors set before us by God, truly becoming partners with God in the Created World of which we are part, bringing God into our world through our actions. Further, this may and undoubtedly will require ***soft souls*** to stand alone while others act in a way that does not conform to this ideal, both within individual faith communities and when we consider our larger family of humanity, the collective of which we are all ultimately part. In the Talmud, we see this sentiment expressed in Shabbat 88a as follows when discussing people who "go in complete faith,"

> The Rabbis taught in a Baraita: Those who suffer insult from others and do not insult the others; those who hear others disgrace them but do not reply; those who do God's will because of love and are happy in any suffering that may result; about them we are taught, And they who love God will be as the sun that goes out in its might.

That is to say that the challenge is clearly acknowledged, but perhaps it is specifically these people who are up to it. Think of all of the people we know who would never want to inflict the pain on others they know all too well. These are often the bullied ones, who become advocates for those who are bullied; these are the abused women who open and maintain shelters for others; and so on. There are so many who are strengthened by these experiences, albeit they would not have chosen them; but so many of these strong soft souls have and do change our world every day, benefitting so many others.

Our soft souls have so much to teach all of us, as we see in these familiar lyrics from "For Good" from **Wicked**:

> I'm limited
> Just look at me
> I'm limited
> And just look at you; You can do all I couldn't do
> Glinda
> So now it's up to you
> For both of us
> Now it's up to you
>
> I've heard it said
> That people come into our lives for a reason
> Bringing something we must learn
> And we are led
> To those who help us most, to grow
> If we let them
> And we help them in return

Well, I don't know if I believe that's true
But I know I'm who I am today
Because I knew you...

I have been changed for good

It well may be
That we will never meet again
In this lifetime
So let me say before we part
So much of me
Is made of what I learned from you
You'll be with me
Like a handprint on my heart
And now whatever way our stories end
I know you have re-written mine
By being my friend...

Who can tell if I've been
Changed for the better?
I do believe I have been
Changed for the better

And because I knew you...
I have been changed for good... (40)

Here is a beautiful expression how two souls can influence and change each other "for good" as a result of an intentional and sincere impact, while navigating the rough vicissitudes of life. If we could all do this in our laboratories, wherever we find them, then perhaps we could take the ways we have been changed "for good" and use that to bring more changes about in our rough world, as a tribute to the kind and gentle connections we have had in our lives.

We must be the soft souls who show others by the very example of our lives and actions how to care and be concerned, how to be compassionate and empathetic. We must shine forth as the sun and persevere in our **Shlichut** to bring kindness, compassion and so much else into our world by our personal example and using the lessons we have learned. In so doing, we bring God into the world in a most palpable manner, emulating God's characteristics and sharing God's pain in confronting the rough winds that we must weather in our journey through the world in which we are all collectively and necessarily invested.

Questions for Continued Thought and Discussion:

1. As we asked in the beginning of this chapter, how do we have sympathy for and 'tolerate' minimally as well as love and cherish maximally the other who is not tolerant of us?

2. What would you do to try to convince another that you were right in a given situation if you truly believed that to be the case? Where does caring for a friend and wanting the best for that friend turn into something more dangerous and insidious and how do we prevent that from happening?

3. Do you consider yourself to be a soft soul? Do you know someone who you would consider to be a soft soul? What do you think is so difficult and challenging for that person (perhaps you) to get through life and our world on a daily basis?

4. What is the abuse of aspect of our lives today that you find most troubling? Why? What can you do to improve the situation?

XI. The Greatest Teacher of All – The Power Above Us All

Moshe said to God, "Behold, when I come to the Children of Israel and say to them, 'The God of your forefathers has sent me to you,' and they say to me 'What is That One's name?' what shall I say to them?" God answered Moshe, "I Shall Be As I Shall Be." And God said, "So shall you say to the Children of Israel"

Exodus/Shemot 3: 13 - 15

One of the ongoing struggles articulated throughout this collection of writings is to balance the notion that among our many differences, some of us believe in God and some of us do not. Virtually every person, if not every single human being, has probably addressed the notion of God at least conceptually at some point, whether they accept, reject, or question the presence of the Divine in their lives. Certainly amongst the teachers and personalities already discussed in these essays, there is a marked variation regarding how each one incorporates God, as either a transcendent or imminent presence, or some combination of these facets, into one's life. How do we accommodate these many different inclinations and belief systems regarding the presence of the Divine in these discussions, acknowledging that while some of the lessons and quandaries presented here are universally shared, the most basic and fundamental underpinnings of what we ultimately believe about each other and ourselves are not necessarily so?

In my teaching and lecturing, I have often dealt with this important dilemma in the following way. I begin with the disclaimer and affirmation that personally, I do believe in God and further I recognize that many of us, that is, the members of our collective community of humanity as well as individual religious groupings, are not yet sure about our beliefs. Some of us believe or affirmatively know that we do not believe in God. In Jewish teachings and sources, God is referred to in so many different ways, accommodating the various attributes and aspects of God's total being, many of which may evoke different responses from so many of us. While Hinduism, for example, acknowledges as many as 3,000 of these different attributes, Judaism and its sources utilize seventy different names of God to reflect so many facets of this complex yet, amazingly singular Being.

Within these different names and aspects of God are found various categorizations of God's involvement in our lives. One schematic that I have used is that some of these names or aspects refer to God as the Creator of All Beings, others refer to God as Source, motivating and causing all to come into being; and yet others refer to God as Force that may act within and upon all that is. Here, there are three different general approaches to help us speak about the ineffable, namely God, as the beginning of all that is, as the sources from which all comes and evolves, or as the force behind it all. I have found that this continuum of possibilities resonates with many more individuals who may not be quite sure or who cannot yield to The Power Above for whatever set of reasons. I find that this enables discussion about the God concept with more people, acknowledging and accommodating their different perspectives regarding God or the force that none of us can aptly explain or prove to one another.

Many years ago, I was having a conversation with a friend's parent who was a psychiatrist. He did not believe in God and was very puzzled as to how I could do so. He and I once sat down to discuss this and he began by asking me outright how I could believe in "something" for which I had no "proof." I was still in my late teens at the time, but on this I was very clear nonetheless. So I began with a simple question, which I put to him as follows, "How do you think that everything we know to be began?" He explained some aspects of what we understood to be a scientific explanation of the beginnings of the Universe, somewhere between evolution and the Big Bang. I then continued to ask, "So where did that come from?" or "What came before that?" Finally, we got to the point where my friend's parent responded, "I don't know." At that moment I proposed that the last unanswered question is what I attribute to God, the Beginning of All That Is. He did not agree with me but did better understand how I, within such an approach, perceived all that is and The Creator that brought it to be.

I have since used this routine repeatedly with many other people and found it to resonate on different levels. We do not all speak about and accept belief in God, but at some point, we all throw our hands up and just do not know how else to explain how all that we know to be came into being. For some of us, this conversation comes to the dead end of the ultimate unanswered question, while for others we acknowledge that our *faith* (perhaps *leap of faith*) kicks in at that point. I have always been struck by the wording of the **Thirteen Principles of Faith** that has evolved from the teachings of Maimonides. Many Jews recite the formula of this wording daily as part of the regimen of prayers that are stated and pondered, and even more study this text at some point in their lives, with each phrase beginning with the words ***I believe with complete faith that ...*** It is important to note that these particular statements of "affirmation" are not about what we *know* to be true, but rather what we fundamentally *believe* to be so as we wade through life. Further in this schema, what one *believes* will ultimately inform what one comes to know as truth.

Lest we think that this processing is limited to people of faith, let us consider that scientists and mathematicians do not in fact operate in all that different a manner. For example, Stephen W. Hawking has certainly been a powerful force in this discussion in the scientific community and beyond about how all that is came to be. In fact, he has been identified as one of, if not the most brilliant mind/s of our tine, formulating and using equations, reasoning and many tools at his disposal to try to articulate the *how* of all that has come to be in the first place. In the introduction to one of Hawking's books, in fact his treatise at the time, **A Brief History of Time** (New York: Bantam Books, 1988), Carl Sagan writes as follows:

> This is also a book about God ... or perhaps about the absence of God. The word God fills these pages. Hawking embarks on a quest to answer Einstein's famous question about whether God had any choice in creating the universe. Hawking is attempting as he explicitly states, to understand the mind of God. (41)

Certainly throughout time, we have been attempting to understand the mind of God and God's sense of purpose as has already been articulated in these discussions. When we ponder the vastness of our universe and our part in it, the desire to acquire such an understanding is nature. Further, as we confront the injustices that will undoubtedly confront us through the course of our lives or inequities in the balance of our existence or ultimate questions to be answered, we are even more driven to try to come to some type of resolution. This attempt is as eternal as is the record of our very being. In fact, it is marked as an identifying core feature of the very nature of humanity.

Do you think that Moshe really received an answer that was satisfactory in the question he puts to God in the quoted text at the beginning of this chapter? Is the way of the scientists as reflected in the work of so many any more clear and proven and satisfactory to all?

Consider these statements:

> When the answer is simple, God is speaking. (Albert Einstein)
>
> Man cannot fully ascertain God for God is so complete and God's complete nature is quite simple. (<u>The Way of God</u>, Rabbi Moshe Chaim Luzzato)

Einstein's pithy statement is well known and says so much in so few words. On the other hand, Luzzato (Ramchal) explains at great length how the human mind is compartmentalized and therefore, God's all-encompassing integration of all elements into a simplistic whole is not comprehensible to the human mind (42). One can clearly understand how this must be so frustrating to so many people of reason. How can we, as thinking, logical human beings accept that God's complexity is not known to us because in truth God's being is pure simplicity!

Is this angst resulting from not finding such ultimate answers not shared by mathematicians, philosophers, artists and others as well? Consider, for example, that in reality, no one can aptly and definitively identity the complete identity and essence of PI in mathematics, every defined set is representative of an absolute sense of reality, a philosophical construct will have inherent limits and boundaries in terms of absolute understanding, and so forth. Perhaps, just perhaps, this is the very essence of one of the most important lessons that God is imparting to each and every one of us through different venues, fields of endeavors, various frames of scholarship, and means of communication – the need to accept and understand that limits and boundaries are as much a truism in our world as is our need to discern and identify them and our desire to know and "own" them, much less entertain the notion of reaching or even moving beyond them.

Years after Moshe's challenge in trying to communicate the essence and identity of God, we are still confronted by the frustration of this search, as exemplified by Ecclesiastes/**Kohelet**'s statement that

> I have seen the tasks, which God has given to all people to be concerned with. God has made every thing good in its time; also God has set the world in the heart of man, so that no person can find out the work that God made from the beginning to the end. (Chapter 3, verses 10 – 11)

As we have already indicated, it is often accepted that this book of Kohelet was penned and/or inspired by King Solomon/**Shlomo**, clearly someone who was seen as wise and knowledgeable, in fact the wisest man of his generation, as well as one whose wisdom comes to identify him so many years and generations later as we remember him and the legacy he left for all. Later yet, Maimonides, also known as **Rambam**, in the twelfth century writes in his **Mishna Torah** in **Hilchot De'ah** that even if man could come to understand all that there is to know about God and God's realm and activities (and it is clear that we cannot due to the limitations of being human!), we would not have the strength or resources to absorb and use all of this knowledge. In other words, we repeatedly see here and in so many other venues that the only one who can know God must be God! This is reinforced in the work of so many religious thinkers, philosophers, scientists, and others throughout the generations of our collective history and experience. Or as an extremely fraught Hershel states in ultimate frustration in the play and movie, The Quarrel, "If I understood God, I would be God."

What is left for us to do once we come to terms with our own limitations and the fact that we will not conclusively come to fully know God and all that God is, but rather we will each experience God in an individuated and necessarily limited manner? The Hindus choose paths that each person can take, well suited for his or her skill sets and acumen. Kohelet provides us with this own final analysis when we read at the end of his book that

> Let us hear and acknowledge the conclusion of the whole matter. Fear God and keep God's commandments, for this is the whole duty of the human being. (12:13 and Postscript)

With this conclusion, Kohelet in his infinite wisdom and with his myriad of resources yields to God and in doing so simultaneously acknowledges the largess of humanity, as well as its limitations. He is adding his name to the list of those with their individuated experiences of God as indicated in our daily prayer of the ***Amidah*** (remember the listing of the Patriarchs and Matriarchs and each of their experiences of God), as every other searching soul indicated in these essays, and every one of us add our own discernment of God to the larger picture of God's Absolute Oneness!

Think of it this way. In my own teaching, when we get to this point of how one discerns God, I often ask students to explain their best friend to the group of learners of which we are part. One by one, students will speak of qualities of kindness, compassion, love, selflessness, consideration of others and so forth. They will not speak of tangible aspects, such as hair color, quality of voice, how tall they are or other physical characteristics of the person they are discussing. Rather they focus on qualities that they have come to know as real regarding their friend, even though they cannot be touched or "proven," so to speak. So it is with God; within our individuated experience, we will each relate to different aspects of God as our greatest teacher and understand that perhaps the limits of what we cannot tangibly come to know may not be so pivotally important after all.

We see the irony of this realization and its many different meanings in so many facets of life. Consider the many different Twelve Step

Programs that are used for people suffering from various addictions – to smoking, drugs, sex, gambling, and other destructive forces that we have already introduced. After the first step of admitting one's weakness and addiction, the individual in such programs quickly moves to yielding to a Higher Power fairly early in the process of going through the scripted steps. In other words, on one hand is the tangible pull of drugs, alcohol, sex, gambling, and so forth while on the other hand is a pull that involves the intangible leap of faith and yielding to something higher. Eventually and quickly enough a few steps later, this power will be identified as God, consistent with the Christian roots of the system as a strategy for coming to terms with human frailty and reality. As the individual progresses through the structured journey of the Twelve Step Program, limitations are acknowledged, a Higher Source turned to, and a group found to validate the humanity and potential of the individual. Further, the humility that the participant will have to attain in understanding that one cannot come to full and absolute knowledge about one self any more than one can about The Creator is part of what leads adherents of such programs to "take one day at a time" because ultimately, that is the best any of us can do.

Parenthetically, it must be noted that this does play out somewhat differently for Christians and Jews as Christians can come to "know" God through their acceptance of Jesus in their lives and identification with saints. Jews do not have this option and are left with the questions as indicated elsewhere in these essays. However, the role of faith in all of these journeys should not be minimized.

When one considers the best that a religious community can be, does it not serve these very purposes? Assuming we do not devolve as self-identified fundamentalist extremists (as was discussed in an earlier essay), the best these groups can offer is validation, identity, support from a Higher Being and the comfort of an embracing group. As we learned earlier, God shows these groups and individuals how to care and provide for each other, through actions such as clothing the naked, visiting the sick, comforting the mourners, and burying the dead, among so many other actions that allow us to show the best of humanity, both the individuals and communities that are part of it.

This is precisely what Harold Kushner speaks about in When Bad Things Happen to Good People (New York: Schocken Books, 1981). When difficult situations present, these are opportunities for the best of humanity to come shining through, and it is here, says Kushner and so many others, that we discern and see the presence of God. It is at just such moments that we hope that we learn what to do from the Higher Being/Source/Force that guides and instructs us all, in one way or another one. If we do not come to know God completely and totally, we acquire knowledge of facets of God through our own actions and involvement with and for others, modeled on those God has already shown us.

Also, implicit in these pages is the idea that there is not only one strategy to be utilized in coming to such a place in one's life. Every ***Pesach***/Passover we are reminded in so many different ways that we each come to our realizations about God, self and community in our own ways, whether we identify with the Four Sons (Children) and the different ways in which they ask questions and find solutions to their quandaries or if we feel comforted by the fact that we need them, or if the physical symbols used as we reenact the drama of leaving Egypt teach us the important message of this time more than the words of the Haggadah, itself. God, in whatever form or function one may accept the Being or Concept, teaches us through God's many different facets and paths that we too, being created in the image of God have many different characteristics and aspects in each one of us. If we pay attention, there is so much we can learn from each other and various perspectives that come into our lives.

There is a wonderful story attributed to Rabbi Avraham Yeshaya Karelitz, known as the *Hazon Ish*, who lived and taught through the first half of the twentieth century that shows how each of us can learn from every person, if we are paying attention. The story shows us that Oprah Winfrey's dream and the child who asks "What was I sent here to teach you?" as well as the lessons learned from the various personalities in these writings and the people who are sitting to the right and left of us in our daily lives are all our potential teachers, as we are for them.

The story goes like this. The *Hazon Ish* was a very respected teacher (Rav) and had many students who were fiercely dedicated to him and learned daily from his lessons (*shiyurim*). When he would teach, students would come from all over, near and far, to hear his words of wisdom. It was the custom then, as it still is in places, for respected students of Torah to rise when an honored student or teacher enters the room. One day, as the *Hazon Ish* was teaching, an individual appeared at the door. The *Hazon Ish* stopped his lesson and waited for the gentleman to take a seat. Since their respected teacher halted his lessons, the many students present also stood and waited for the newcomer to be seated, which was also a customary act of respect towards the one from whom one learned.

However, an air of puzzlement began to spread across the room as people realized that they were standing and waiting for a rather bedraggled and disoriented fellow to find his place. Clearly this was not a Torah scholar or student of repute. So why was their respected teacher waiting? Who was this man? After the lesson, a few students ventured hesitantly to ask their venerated teacher why he had responded as he had to this individual. Their teacher looked at them and gently responded by explaining that this person suffered so terribly from illness and ongoing challenges that it was an incredible chore for him just to get up in the morning and get dressed and be part of the community. Nonetheless, he did just that every day. So, taught the ***Hazon Ish***, no matter how poorly I am feeling on a given day I think of this man. He is an inspiration, he is my teacher and I learn important lessons from him every day. It is for this reason that I stand out of respect for my honored teacher!

Clearly this scholar knew very well what this person was sent to teach him. We are taught in the Talmud that this is one of the greatest gifts given to us by God, our differences and variations, including even, and sometimes, especially, our challenges and obstacles to overcome. There is even a special blessing/***Beracha*** that we say when we see someone who is physically different. We thank God for creating so many different human beings. We may not always think of these differences as those we would choose for ourselves. Nonetheless, we accept that on some level, Our Creator chose these people as well as the lessons they teach us for us to learn from them. It is our initiative and acknowledgement that will allow them into our lives.

We are acutely aware of, as well as drawn to, heroes in our society who have overcome amazing obstacles in their lives, including the musician who is brilliant and blind or even deaf, the sports figure who had to confront serious and potentially debilitating illness, the writer whose soulful words inspire so many and are produced from within the depths of his or her own suffering, and so forth. What incredible gifts these individuals are able to produce; one must wonder to what degree these gifts and their challenges are correlated. Is it possible that some of these challenges are actually teaching tools or opportunities that are given to us by God?

We have quoted from the Latter Prophets/***Neviim Achronim*** through these essays. Let us stop for a moment and consider that these teachers from long ago had weaknesses and challenges to address as well as their strengths for which they are so known. Most of them did not want to be entrusted with this very serious and awesome responsibility, yet God insisted that these were the right people for their respective positions! Here we learn a critically important aspect of God and how God relates to created beings. God provides the support that is needed by each of these leaders accordingly, as God does for each and every human being, we would hope.

As Moshe Rabbeinu indicated that he could not speak and God promised that Aaron would be his spokesman; and Jeremiah did not know how he would carry on his responsibilities, receiving support as well; so too it was in each case. God communicated with each prophet and leader in the way that was most meaningful and relevant to that person, whether it was through metaphors, diatribes, personal life experience or whatever was needed. The prophets then went on to teach others through these learned tools and skill sets. It is interesting to consider the thought that God understands very well the differences in all created beings, especially as the Creator of those beings. Further, the notion must be considered that while no one of us holds all of the pieces to the big puzzle of life by ourselves, it is to our clear advantage to join together and create community with others in order to put our individual pieces of that puzzle, including our talents, lessons learned and challenges confronted together in order to understand the greater whole of our shared existence. Indeed, we are to consider what it was that each person sent here to teach and learn from each other!

God's different teaching modalities, which match learning modalities of prophets, reflect this puzzle approach. One of the most dramatic techniques employed by God is clearly the prescribed life experience of Hosea as explained in Chapter One, verses 2 – 3:

> God said to Hosea, "Go take a wife of harlotry for yourself and children of harlotry, for the land has committed great harlotry, departing from The Lord." So Hosea went and took Gomer … and she conceived and bore him a son.

God intends to use this experience to show Hosea how God's love for the Jewish nation, the B'nai Yisrael, is so powerful that it continues in spite of the actions and rebellions of this nation. Hosea is to be the prophet that will bring this message to the people entrusted to his care and it is critically important to God that Hosea understands and believes in this message and its lesson. God has chosen, according to the text, to use Hosea's personal life and the very family he will create as the ultimate in object lessons to convey the depth and unconditional nature of this love. While this modality worked for Hosea, God chooses other strategies for different leaders in the Biblical narrative and their individuated needs.

The Talmud uses a practical example to show how this dynamic of variation in experience and response presents in all that God has created and continues to fashion. The metaphor used involves how the human being who mints coins can use a single mold that has been fashioned and produce untold numbers of coins, all exactly alike and indistinguishable from each other. On the other hand, God creates so many human beings, all ***BeTzelem Elokim***, like each other in being created in God's image but vastly different from each other in virtually every other and so many different ways (Sanhedrin 38a). These variations reflect the most profound indication of God's wisdom and foresight. The question is how do we use these variations of human capacity and ability constructively to build and not destroy the world that has been entrusted into our collective care. We must come to terms with the fact that God as the master teacher has chosen to provide us with this great challenge – that of our differences – precisely so that we can learn the most important lesson of how to deal with them and incorporate them into our lives as we build community and learn with and from each other. Ignoring this point and the challenge entailed is missing so much of the raison d'etre of our being part of this world and potentially squandering the opportunity God has given us to do so.

Returning to the initial point of this chapter and other discussions within this collection, one of these most profound variations is how and to what degree we believe. How can there possibly be so many different paths to the Divine, both between various religious traditions as well as within one religious community? This too is part of the wonder and one of the gifts given to us by God, in teaching us how to accept each other as well as ourselves. We are to remember a most compelling lesson from the daily Jewish prayer unit, called the ***Amidah*** or the ***Shemoneh Esrei*** as discussed earlier regarding our individuated experiences of God and God's many different manifestations. It is up to each of us to use our ability of choosing to determine how we will relate to God and in turn bring God and the various facets of God's being and essence into our world through our actions. We will bring different aspects of God into our world in various ways and through different means. Of this, the believers accept that God is profoundly aware.

In Steven Spielberg's <u>Close Encounters of the Third Kind</u> (New York: Dell, 1977), we see this dynamic of varied experience play out, while different perceptions of truth ultimately lead the driven person to the source of that truth. For the purposes of this discussion it is enough to point out that there is a vision, an overwhelming event to which many people are exposed. Some people do not acknowledge it at all for they either do not recognize it or cannot do so. Others are not sure of what they have witnessed and question whether or not to pursue it, deciding not to. Others still are aware of the effects of this occurrence, be it what they have perceived through their eyes or acknowledgement of the burning of their skin that has resulted. At the end, those that feel compelled to follow the experience to its source pursue it. A very few feel so compelled and it is these people that the story traces further and fully develops, both in terms of their individual journeys and how the trajectory of their experiences interface with each other.

One of these people, Roy Neary, has followed the different manifestations and perceptions of what was occurring to its very source. Towards the end of the story, he is confronted by one of the scientists who have their own understanding of what is going on that is related to his search:

> "You tell me," [Lacombe] said in slow, careful English, "you imagined this mountain before you had discovered its existence? It manifested itself to you in many ways. Shadows on the wall, ideas, geometric images that to you, Mr. Neary, seemed like progress toward the familiar but sadly and for so long without any meaning until, finally, it came to you. And it was right!" (43)

While many might, and indeed do dismiss seemingly strange occurrences and signs, some feel compelled to follow them. The question is can those that do so make sense of them? What happens if they cannot; what happens to those journeys? Can our community, our collective, handle different and individuated understandings and journeys of this nature; that is to say can we all consider a phenomenon and translate or interpret it differently, according to our own place in the universe? Finally, how do we build a community of appreciation and acceptance of many different people with their varied perceptions of the Divine and its manifestations in our world, which we all experience in such individuated manners? How do we share these various perceptions of truth with each other in a meaningful, kind and compassionate manner, with a willingness to learn from and with others and expand our own reality in doing so?

Remember our friend, *Avraham Aveinu* and his incredible journey? Certainly he was drawn towards a source, towards God. How many different manifestations might he have perceived before he followed the voice he heard? *Moshe Rabbeinu* certainly discerned God's presence and instruction through many different means and felt compelled to follow the clues placed before him. We could say the same for each of the personae indicated in the texts of our heritage and in the examples provided in these pages. Undoubtedly we see remarkable variation and use of so many different modalities in God's instruction and involvement with these many different people. In providing such individuated approaches and experiences, God is showing compassion and understanding of the highest degree for the many different human beings that are part of God's Created World. It is this quality of God that is acknowledged and repeatedly cited in the daily prayers and core texts of the Jewish nation as well as in other faith communities.

There is a wonderful text in Talmud, towards the very beginning of this voluminous tome, which conveys perhaps the most powerful aspect and picture of God regarding this compassion and how God acts towards the beings that God has created. In Berachot 7a, we read as follows:

> How do we know that God prays? Because it is said, "I will bring the people to My sanctified mountain and make them joyful in the house of My prayer."... What does God pray for? ... "May it be My will that My mercy conquer My anger and that My mercy overcome all of My strictest attributes and that I behave towards My children with the strictest attribute of mercy and that for their sake I go beyond the required boundary of judgment."

In this text, we see that God so highly values compassion and that it should be at the root and the most salient motivating factor for every aspect of God's involvement with us, including judgment. What an incredible lesson for us to apply in our lives by learning from this example provided by The Creator according to the teaching of the Talmud. By accepting each other and acting towards one another

206

with compassion, we are emulating the very actions of The Creator and bringing God into the world in so modeling our behaviors. In this way, we all come to the table with our various experiences of God, our different talents, our challenges and the lessons we learn from them, and the many other aspects of our reality provided for us by The Creator and help to put the large puzzle of our collective existence together in a manner that reflects the best of what God has provided for us. Our success in doing this best reflects the success of God as the Ultimate Teacher of us all.

Questions for Continued Thought and Discussion:

1. What powerful lessons do you believe that you have learned from what you know to be true in terms of our existence in our shared Universe?

2. What powerful lessons do you believe that you have learned from what you do not know and cannot prove to be true – those aspects of life that you find most perplexing and frustrating?

3. What sense do you have of God in any form from Higher Being to Source to Force and how does this help you discern all of the above lessons; or if not, why is it not sufficient?

XII. Achdut: Accepting and Appreciating The Gifts We All Bring

For the misdeed we have committed before You, God, through judgment [and lack of acceptance of others and their differences], forgive us and pardon us and allow us to atone

Vidui prayer of confession, Yom Kippur

Several years ago, when I was teaching a class at a Community Jewish Day School, one of my students approached me and asked if we could chat for a few moments. I responded affirmatively and asked her what was so troubling at that time. Her eyes began to tear up as she explained that she felt horribly guilty about everything. I was somewhat stunned, as I had no idea what she was talking about and asked her what she meant. She then began to explain that as she listened to the various religious struggles of different members of the class (which was somehow related to what we were doing together academically, as is often the case), she realized that she was not at all religious, that is not to say according to the parameters of the discussion at hand. She proceeded to describe how some students were wrestling with various aspects of Halachic observance, such as how strictly they should observe Kashrut, whether or not to wear a Kipah and Tzitzit at all times, how observant one should be regarding Shabbat and so forth.

She continued by explaining that she came from a non-observant home and that she felt guilty regarding the issues she was struggling with, for example, whether to light candles on Shabbat or other such seemingly minimal decisions. We then began to speak about what Shabbat meant to her and she told me the following story. She shared that she had been visiting the nursing home where her grandmother lived every Saturday afternoon for many years to spend

208

time with her Bubby and her friends. Some time ago, her Bubby had died but she still felt a connection and responsibility to other residents in the nursing home and therefore had continued her Saturday afternoon visits. I was so touched by this incredible act of *chesed* shown by this young lady and asked her if she had ever stopped to consider what this action meant to those who looked forward to her weekly visit.

This act was so kind, so respectful, so *mitzvah* laden, so Jewish! We could all learn a great deal from this special Jewish teenager. I often find that people confuse and interface the terms ***too religious, too observant, too Jewish*** and ***too Orthodox.*** While this young lady may not be Orthodox, what could be more Jewish than to make this decision regarding how to spend her Saturday afternoons, her Shabbat? I love the Chasidic notion that every Jew does many Mitzvot every day and if we were to focus on this aspect of the members of our community, then we might find we share more than we might think at first glance. We would certainly appreciate the gifts, talents, and the values we all bring to the table of Jewish community, even in the face of those who bristle at the notion of "big tent Judaism," defining who we are as Jews in the broadest and most expansive manner possible within the confines of being Jewish.

In doing so, we add so much. Just like our friend, Reb Zusya who learned that God wanted for him to be the best Zusya he could possibly be, this student learned that she should work on being the best person she could and was meant to be, and not judge herself by standards maintained by another. Of course, then there is that matter of balance again. Can we entertain the notion that "being the best" will be different for each of us and that we need to value the best in others according to their own benchmarks and the ones ordained for them by God, not those we would impose on them as my Israeli friend from earlier and so many others might have it. But, you might ask, how can we be so sure that we should pull back and yield to someone else's sense of right? What if they are "wrong," really misguided in terms of how we are supposed to live according to a prescribed code such as **Halacha**? But then again, are we not taught that while we are all striving to live as we should, we are all "not there yet?" In such a situation are we yielding to the other or to God and God's plan for the other? Remember, we learn in the Pesach experience as we read through the Haggadah and in our prayers that we need those that build our institutions and community structures as well as those that will use them. In our laws about **Tefillah**/prayer and prayer communities, we are taught by Rambam that we need the one who reads Torah and leads the congregational prayer as much as the one who says Amen to the prayers that are led. In other words, we each bring different abilities and gifts to the table of our community and we should learn to respect and value all of these as well as come to an understanding that each of us will be further enriched by the sharing of these different capacities and deeds.

Achdut is an important term, referring to the unit and "coming together" of the various groupings and individuals within the Jewish community. Certainly a correlative unity in our larger world is sought as well. An important aspect of this facilitation of the collective is to recognize our differences and acknowledge as well as appreciate and accommodate them, whether they are related to levels or types of knowledge, religious observance, political beliefs, skills and so forth. While there is so much that we share, there are those components of our being and experience that are differentiated as well. In many, if not most of, the mainstream communities indicated here, this is acknowledged. For the separatists within the streams of each of our faith groupings, this is the very source of what threatens the unity and confluence of all factors of one's existence that are so valued by adherents to this type of life.

We have already referred to the prayer of the **Aleinu** recited in the Jewish community in which we end with the verse from the prophet

Zechariah (14.9) that states "God will be King over all the world, on that day God will be One and God's name will be One." The point could clearly be made that this expresses the most general hopes for unity and shared understanding amongst all peoples and their different orientations and belief systems, as well as the various voices that they hear and present. Yet, one cannot ignore the fact that this can also be read as a significant dividing line that defines and differentiates peoples, including those who do and do not accept a belief in the Divine and other components of this line in the sand, so to speak. In fact, as we look at the entirety of this particular prayer, we are confronted with several statements affirming that difference and informing us that the Jewish way is the best way, or for many, the only way. When one examines the history of this prayer and its development as well as how it came to be included in our daily prayers, one is challenged to acknowledge the nature of this irony. While so much of this **Tefillah** emphasizes clearly the difference between the Jewish belief in God and that belief amongst other nations and peoples, this verse from Zechariah states the hope that all people of the world will come together and accept this belief in the One and Only One who is outside of the confines of the reality of the human condition, and hopefully Compassionate and Concerned for all. So what exactly is the nature of this hope? Is it a unified and shared hope or is it something else? How do we resolve the inherent conflict found in this statement of faith and belief, that is to say, does it unify or divide?

Belief in **Yichud HaShem**, the acceptance of the Absolute Oneness of God, is a central aspect and foundational belief of Judaism and all of the components that define it, remembering that we may all perceive this Absolute Oneness and its many facets in different ways. In fact, much discussion about the formulation and elements of the Aleinu is so wrapped up with the focus on this concept. To be sure, this is also the case with so many of the prayers that are an intrinsic part of daily Jewish lives, certainly the **Shema** among others – Listen carefully Israel, the Lord our God, the Lord is One!

So we have to honestly consider how we can even begin a discussion of the striving for unity of all the peoples of the world when not all people share this notion of the Oneness of God. How can we talk about achieving a sense of shared understanding when there is truly so much that does in fact divide the people of the world, not to mention the members of our own faith community? If we do not acknowledge and accept the differences that define us individually, we will never be able to come together in a meaningful way based on what we share. How do we balance our understanding of desired unity with this acknowledgement and acceptance of differences? To do so is critical as we attempt to build bridges and arenas of understanding and shared acceptance both within the Jewish community among out own groupings as well as among the **Umot HaOlam**, the different nations that are included in the world in which we live. How do we initiate and implement such a process? How do we listen to and share with others while maintaining and not compromising the standards we hold to be true for ourselves?

We can and should begin by looking at our words and the process of thought that produces this. After all, it is such words and thoughts that are collectively the most important tool of communication with others. We must always remain cognizant of the power of our words to build up as well as break down, echoing the statement of **Kohelet** (3:7). We noted in the beginning of this chapter the text in the **Vidui,** the Confessional Prayer of **Yom Kippur** in which we acknowledge the many ways in which we have failed ourselves, each other and God as we read:

Al Heit SheHatanu Lefanecha B'Fililut

For the misdeed we have committed before You, God, through judging others.

It is significant to note that the word ***fililut*** comes from the Hebrew root, *f.l.l*, the same root from which the word for ***Tefillah***, or prayer comes. We need to begin this consideration of how we regard others with an acute awareness of the power of words as tools of building as well as destruction. What do we say to others? How do we acknowledge the gifts and beliefs that they bring to the table? Why do we speak as we do with others? What is our purpose in speaking and sharing with others? Just as important, how do we process the words we hear from others?

Years ago, one of the most powerful experiences I have ever had in Israel was at a special institute named ***Yakir***. One of the important and poignant things done at this place in Jerusalem (the City of Peace, according to the meaning of its name) is to bring Muslims and Jews together to study shared texts together, respecting our differences while celebrating shared heritage. I spent a full morning there concentrating on the story of ***Akedat Yitzchak***, the narrative of Avraham and his readiness to sacrifice his son Yitzchak to God, which is familiar to virtually every Jew as well as many other members of other faith communities. My Muslim study partner, a woman from East Jerusalem, was also familiar with the narrative from her own faith literature, the Koran (Chapter 37: 97 – 111). However in this retelling of the narrative, there was one quite notable variation in her understanding and knowledge of the story, namely that it was not Yitzchak that Avraham was ready to sacrifice to God, thus cementing the tie between the three eternally but rather Yishmael, Avraham's son by Hagar. She held her faith literature sources as sacrosanct and I held mine as being so for me.

One of the important eternal truths to know about Islam is that they hold that their scripture, the Koran along with its supportive text, is the most correct distillation of the original word of God or Allah, including some texts and ideas found in Torah (as well as later texts, including Talmudic passages occasionally) and in all cases the most accurate and correct message from the Divine. Islam, itself, is taken to be the most perfect religion as reflected in the following statement translated from Al-Maida 5:3

> This day, have those who reject faith given up all hope of your religion: yet fear them not but fear Me. This day have I perfected your religion for you completed my favor upon you and have chosen for you Islam as your religion. (44)

Therefore, if I were to claim "you are wrong" to my study partner regarding her fundamental truth that it was Yishmael who was the subject of this critical narrative, this would have been the end of the session whether or NOT she might feel and even state such to me. Rather, I knew this truism about her belief and simply indicated that on this difference we would agree to disagree. Nonetheless, we could share what Avraham's hope and intention must have been for his children and the many nations that they would father, and he therefore would have begun ***ipso facto***.

My goal was not to change her belief system nor was I focused on convincing her that she was wrong. My goal, rather, was to say, "Okay, this is what I believe (or know) to be true given my Eternal Truths and this is what you believe (or know) to be true given your Eternal Truths. Now what do we do in terms of figuring out how to co-exist? What lessons are there in the life and tests of Avraham Aveinu from which we can learn, in terms of his concern for his sons, his negotiations with Lot for land and his absolute faith in God as well as so much else? How do we consider the option of how we live in our world simultaneously, sharing where we can and parting ways peaceably where we must? Finally, how do we teach others by our example in accomplishing this shared and cooperative venture?"

After our study together and "lack of resolution," with respect and regard for each other, we hugged each other and each went our separate ways with wishes for Shalom and Salaam.

Remember Hillel's lesson of ***Elu v'Elu***, these and those are the words of God. Further, remember that the reason we yield to Hillel is that Hillel regarded and respected the words of those with whom he disagreed and even presented them first. Recognizing that we do not all have the same "comfort zones" in terms of such dialogue, whether within our own communities or among the various communities that compose the family of humanity, if we would each at least consider such an approach, think of the bridges that we could collectively build. Further, we really might just learn something new and remarkable from others given that those ideas too come from God or … just because!

In attempting the accomplishment of such an agenda of effective interaction and communication, we must recognize that we all have our own Eternal Truths, those foundational beliefs that we hold as fundamental in explaining our understanding of the world and our part in it. These Eternal trusts define a given people and the adherents to a specific faith, as well as individuals and their approach to the Universe of which we are all part. How is it possible that these Eternal Truths are not the same for all people? On the other hand, think about it – how is it even possible that these Eternal Truths could be the same or even remotely similar for each and every person!

Let us return for a moment to the following statement from Peskita de Rav Kahana 12:25: "Do not be misled if you hear many voices. Know that I am the One God for each of you." As with any text, we learn that there are different ways in which to read and understand such a statement. On one end of the spectrum, one could surmise that the "many voices" are detracting one from understanding the

Oneness of God. Yet, by inclusion of the words "for each of you" is it not possible that we are being told that while God speaks with One Voice, we as human beings hear and distill the words of God through many different processes and understandings. Thus, could we not make the case that God is aware and even accepting of the fact that we have our own means of interpreting the words of God and that in doing so, we have contributions to make as we (and if we in fact can) join our hands and hearts together, each gently and carefully adding his or her part of the message indicated for all of us collectively by The Creator of us all. If God understands that one communication can be distilled as "many voices," then why can we not come to learn to do the same? How strong is the responsibility we all share to do so? Here is yet another way we can all work to live up to the standard of truly being made in the image of God, **BeTzelem Elokim.**

Philosophical discourse and sharing such as that informed by our textual legacy indicated here is an important tool in itself. What techniques and models do we have to help us engage in such process within our Jewish community as well as with other communities of Faith? Clearly the case could be made that this is yet one of, if not the most significant one of the "gifts of the Jews" to our world community, with due respect to Tom Cahill. The good news is that at this point in time, as our world continues to become increasingly polarized in so many different ways, more and more people are agreeing to come together to the table, with their own beliefs and Eternal Truths, with the agenda of sharing them with others and learning about these other perspectives of our world and our lives. We have already noted how we can, if we are interested and seek them out, read of such groups throughout the United States, Israel, Canada and so many other places. Sadly, however, even though we are hearing and reading about these efforts even more, they still do not get nearly enough press time, which is otherwise absorbed by the devastating effects of not being able to achieve such a goal as listening to and sharing with others, who may not believe as we do.

We all know the story of the Rabbi who had two of his congregants confront him with conflicting views of the same issue. The Rabbi listened to the first congregant state their case and then thoughtfully paused after which he replied, "You are right." After this, the second congregant approached the Rabbi with his absolutely opposite point of view on the same issue. After listening just as thoughtfully to the second congregant, the Rabbi replied, "You are right." The Rabbi's wife had been listening to these discussions and then asked her husband how it was possible that both of the congregants could be right with such disparate points of view. To this the Rabbi replied, "My dear, you too are right!" Surely this Rabbi understood that while God speaks, we hear and discern differently. He did not need to declare one person "right" and the other "wrong," nor did he compromise his own standards or values by listening carefully for the "truth" in each of the words of those who came to him. What an important lesson we learn from this little story. It is the lesson of "***Elu vElu,***" these are the words of God and these are also the words of God. We should challenge ourselves to truly listen to them all!

So, for those of us who accept the premise explored and set forth here, where are the opportunities to teach our students and exemplify for our communities the possibilities of such interaction with those who do not agree regarding important details about our individual Eternal Truths? Simply, such opportunities are right in front of us, if we can create the appropriate climate. Further, we need to agree that our Jewish sources and texts teach important values about our *Achrayut*, our responsibility to build such bridges of understanding and acceptance in spite of, perhaps even because of our differences.

To be sure, there are many references to the harm that **Sinat Hinam**, senseless and profoundly hurtful hatred between people, has done and continues to cause in our world. We are even taught by our sages that the destruction of our Second Temple and so much else that has been devastating in our history was due to this senseless hatred between people.

We as Jews accept that all of us, all members of the Jewish community as well as all members of the worldwide community are created **BeTzelem Elokim**, in the image of God. In terms of these shared roots, we understand that all of us are created by The Creator, and that we are to recognize and respect the spark of The Divine in all of humanity. This can often be quite a challenge, to acknowledge that we are all created by the same Creator while that Creator formed each of us with different qualities and characteristics and beliefs. Further, throughout Jewish texts and sources we find the stated goal that we must learn how to achieve the ideal of this mutual acceptance and appreciation of each other. Both **Ahavat Yisrael** and **Ahavat Olam**, love of Jews and love of all human beings respectively, are stated values and central elements for the people of Israel.

Some years ago, I was in Jerusalem with the Women in Green on Tisha B'Av, the day we commemorate so much destruction and pain in Jewish history. What an amazing group! After the reading of **Eicha**, the Book of Lamentations, we all rose as one community, including secular and religious, Reform and Hassidic, Conservative and Orthodox, Ethiopian and Russian, Iranian and Moroccan, Reconstructionist and Traditional, Israeli and those of us not living in **Medinat Yisrael**, Jews and a few non-Jews expressing their solidarity, and as one body, we encircled the **Chotsot HaIr**, the walls of the old city of Jerusalem, after which we converged at the **Kotel HaMaaravi**, the Western Wall, with thousands of others who had not marched with us. Our purpose was to pray, to think, and to just be… a community, a **Kehilah** – one that spanned miles, time frames, political beliefs, cultural boundaries and ideological definitions.

For that night, for that moment in time, at that precise universal place and space in which we all felt the pain of what we as a people, both as a consolidated group and as part of the world wide community have lost, there was great reason to rejoice in the hope created by the oneness and the unity of that moment. We are taught that the true miracle of the receiving of Torah that God was gracious enough to bestow upon us was that we, the members of **Klal Yisrael**, received it *"belev echad u'bekol echad,"* with one unified heart and one unified voice in a relatively small physical area at one time. That walk around the walls of our beloved **Yerushalayim** was truly, I felt, such a moment. God must have been smiling about what was occurring at that juncture in time through the tears over what had happened in the past and what we know all too well would continue to happen in the future. This experience was as close to idyllic as I have ever been, but it was only for a few hours. How do we and can we sustain such unity for an extended period of time?

We have spoken about the profundity of God's prayer that God's *midat rachamim*, that measure of compassion and caring that is boundless, will be the most important one God uses when acting as judge of all beings (Berachot 7a). We have also considered the Talmudic discussion in Sotah 14a, in which we are taught that the very way in which we "walk with God" is through these actions, such as visiting the ill, comforting the mourner, burying the dead, and clothing the one in need of clothes. Actions of kindness and caring, of *chesed*, are what unite us with God and ultimately with each other. It is this that our Prophets, our *Nevi'im* hoped for so profoundly and its absence that they mourned so bitterly. The actions such as those of my student who continued going to the nursing home every Saturday (Shabbat) after the death of her grandmother; or those of the prophet Hosea in loving his wife and children; or those many *mitzvot* and deeds of *chesed* that we are taught that Jews do every day; or those random deeds of kindness we witness amongst so many of humanity can and do indeed change so much!

What an amazing thought – through the doing of such actions, we effect the repairing of our world, *Tikkun Olam*, and in so doing unite with the Creator, our God – as spoken of in the words of Zechariah, and bring the gifts we all have to our larger world community! As we all continue to try to dialogue with as well as listen to each other, we can hopefully find and tap the goodness in all those created *BeTzelem Elokim* and accept our differences while acknowledging what unites us. On that day may God's name be One and may our entire community acknowledge this Oneness – through our different understandings, the gifts we all bring to the collective of humanity, our many vices, and certainly our deeds of *chesed* as we care for and show concern for each other in ways that we have learned from God and with and from each other.

Questions for Continued Thought and Discussion:

1. Think of a successful model of a cooperative community that works well as a unit and describe it.

2. Think of an unsuccessful model of a community that does not work well and may even be destructive and describe it.

3. Now, compare these two models and note which characteristics the successful model has.

4. What do you think is the most powerful question in this chapter and how do you propose we address the challenge it places before us?

XIII. How To Build our Community: A Model from the Past and Reality of the Present

Philosophy is to be studied not for the sake of any definite answers to its questions, since no definite answers can, as a rule, be known to be true, but rather for the sake of the questions themselves.
Bertrand Russell (45)

This statement may indeed seem out of place here, but the point is that it is very much appropriately cited. Why, you may ask? Because – the reading of this book does not end with only the reading, with only the thoughts, with the myriad of questions and the plethora of possible approaches! No, this is not a philosophical treatise, but rather a collection of thoughts that we share and process in hopes of working to make our world a better place; our communities more intentional and inclusive; and our actions more focused and purposeful. The model that we will consult in trying to do so comes from the Talmud itself and clearly, answers are sought and proposed and discussed and accepted, for the sake of community and the individuals that are part of it.

Clearly we are sharing what we think and processing our ideas about challenges and realities of our existence and insofar as we are about what we think, this is philosophical, to be sure. However, while we are mostly interested in the questions, we are equally interested in approaches they may and will suggest for our lives to try to make our world a better place. At this time in which we all live and share our universe, where there is so much unrest and fractured pieces of our world, there is simultaneously great cause for hope with so many initiatives and millions of people working to truly make our universe a better place for all. This is our focus for this last discussion in this collection of writings and thoughts.

Many of us do actually believe that the work we are to do in this world, which we share, is sanctified and important work. Consider this thought from Rabbi Hayim HaLevi Donin:

> The purpose of holiness permeates all of Jewish religious law, and encompasses every aspect of human concern and experience. We find that Judaism is concerned with
>
> 1. The sanctity of the person,
> 2. The sanctity of time, and
> 3. The sanctity of place.
>
> All of Jewish law can be defined in terms of one or another of these categories. (46)

Imagine if all people of faith would approach the notion set forth in this schematic of beliefs and standards in their lives in this manner. This concept of elevation of the practical details of our lives to a level of greater meeting and purpose has been discussed earlier from an individual point of view.

But at this point, I would like for us to apply this to our sense of how we work together to create a community. Remember the meaning of that prefix, ***com(m)*** as "with" from our earlier discussion! How do we create the community we hope to share – ***with unity***? Unity is ***not*** necessarily indicative of complete agreement in politics, religious expression, ideological approach, and so on. Rather, it is a collective in which we can all agree that the sanctity of the public and shared entity is to the advantage of all of the individuals that are part of it. Clearly, the Jewish Talmud itself continually models this coming together of disparate points of view, difference in practices, working under different authorities. In short, within that community of learning and within the myriad of discussions engaged across miles and generations, there is exactly this model of inclusion of those with whom we do not agree, or as discussed previously, the culture of dialogue and disagreement known in Jewish learning circles as **Tarbut HaMachloket.**

So how exactly does this model work? To explore it, I will rely heavily on **Masechet Hagiga**, that treatise which is dedicated to the offerings that are brought on the three pilgrimage festivals by all of the members of the Nation of Israel. In fact, the very first word of the Tractate is **all**, referring to all members of the community. Next, watch what happens very quickly.

This text begins as follows:

> MISHNA: **All** are bound in the case of appearing in the Temple Courtyard with offerings on the major festivals (Pesach, Shavuot, and Sukkot) except a deaf-mute, a deranged person, a minor, and one of doubtful sex (androgynous) and one of double sex (hermaphrodite), and women and bondsmen who have not been freed, the lame, the blind, the sick and infirmed, the aged, and he who is not able to go upon his feet from Jerusalem to the Temple Courtyard.
>
> Who is the minor who is exempt from appearing in the Temple Courtyard: Every one who is unable to ride on his father's shoulders, and to go up from Jerusalem to the mountain of the Temple. These are the words of the School of Shammai. But the School of Hillel say: Every one who is unable to take hold of his father's hand, and to go up from Jerusalem to the mountain of the Temple, as it is said [Ex. xxiii. 14], "Three times shall there be pilgrimages." (47)

Our use of this Mishna and other texts in this Tractate are for the purpose of discussing the inclusivity of the community. So we are immediately struck by what happens to the use of the word **all**. By the end of the list of all of the exceptions, we have to ask, "Who is left?" So here is the point that I believe is being made in the text. The Hagiga offering which was associated with the Festivals of Pesach/Passover, Shavuot and Sukkot, was to be offered by all members of the community. That being said, only those who were properly prepared and maintaining a certain specified level of ritual purity were obligated to bring these offerings. Therefore, all of the groups indicated are exempt (that is **Patur,** not *Assur* or forbidden, a most important point and distinction to remember) from the requirement of bringing this offering. That being said, how do you exempt someone from such a requirement without excluding them from the community? This is central in any such discussion of Jewish responsibility regarding any aspect of ritual law and must be addressed. Clearly, it is included as a basic challenge in any such discussion in our contemporary times, especially in the more liberal parts of our larger Jewish community.

First of all it is important to understand that there is a distinct difference from being exempt from fulfilling a requirement and being forbidden in doing so. Too often in religious meanderings of what it means to be "in" or "out" of a Jewish community, these two distinct categories are confused and conflated. Lengthy discussions in this Tractate continue to include as a quite prominent side conversation the notion of what is meant in each of these categories and what criteria must be met for one to be included in them, exceptions to the category, hints in the text of the authoritative word of the Torah that leads to these exceptions, and most important, the notion that all categorizations of sub-groups are not merely binary, that is not everyone or every category can or should be reduced to X or not-X. Rather, there is a myriad of "grey zones" in each continuum of identity points that is deliberated in this text. This is as it should be and herein lays an important challenge to our communities in our contemporary times.

What do I mean by this? Immediately on the first page of the Tractate, we ask who is included in the category of one who is not free, the bondsman.

As the Gemara begins its lengthy discussion of conditions and inclusion of those that are obligated to bring the offering of observance, the Hagiga, we read:

> For the sake of the world, it was ordained that the master of the slave shall be compelled to set that slave free for the purpose that this person should be able to marry a free person (and fulfill the obligation of having children), and the slave shall give the master a note for this being set free for the half of his value.

So, here we note the lengths that are employed to have the status of "slave" removed for the purpose of this person being able to fulfill various Mitzvot or deeds and not accept the proscribed exemption from them. Further this is done for no other reason than the most important one of all -- "for the sake of the world." This shows the power of an individual person and their prominence, even when they are "half-servant"!

As we continue learning this text, before we get to the Gemara itself, note that in the text of the Mishna we are already concerned with who is the minor, the **katan**, characterized by who can make the journey through his own physical ability and the degree of help one might need to do so and still be included.

Just as quickly, the next category is introduced in the very beginning of the discussion, namely the person who is blind. What about the person who is blind in only one eye? Does one have to have use of both eyes to be obligated to bring this offering and be part of the community that sees and is seen in the Temple Courtyard during the festivals and their celebration?

As we proceed, let's consider what is stated about the *cheresh*, the deaf-mute on 2b of the text:

> The Mishna taught that the deaf-mute is in the same category as the deranged person and the minor. Just as the deranged person and the minor are not *b'nai de'ah* (mentally competent for this task and its details); so too, the deaf-mute is not mentally competent (for this task and its details). This Mishnah teaches us what we learned in another Mishnah: The deaf-mute of whom the sages speak in all instances is one who cannot hear and cannot speak. This implies that one who speaks but cannot hear or one who hears but cannot speak is obligated to appear in the Temple Courtyard during the festivals.

Therefore, an entire subset of the grouping of *cheresh* is now included in the larger community, fulfilling the prescribed Mitzvah of gathering and bringing of the Hagiga offering. What important lesson do we learn from this about who and what we are as community and the degree to which disabilities or deficits would serve to exclude a member from the larger entity?

Further, please take note what is the context of the discussion. This is not about who is included or not included, but rather who has the obligation to participate in the offering under examination. It is critical to understand that this is the most foundational criterion for these types of deliberations. Additionally, the Rabbis of the Talmud will and often do go to great lengths to try to be as precise as possible with the texts from which these practices evolve and in so doing, include people as much as possible within a variety of set criteria and within the framework of stated exceptions that result.

A wonderful example in the larger Jewish community of this type of reasoning can be found in the beginning of a most important organization that has done wonderful work for so many of our students in so many of our schools during the past four decades, ***Parents for Torah for all Children*** or **P'TACH**.

Consider the following statement that can be found at the website of this important resource for the entire Jewish community: http://www.ptach.org

> ***In 1976, something very special happened to Special Education.***
>
> P'TACH began as an answer to a pressing problem.
>
> Too many Yeshiva students with special learning needs were being left behind.
>
> There were simply no alternatives. P'TACH was created on the simple premise that children with learning differences need a different way to learn. And so, in 1976 "Parents For Torah For All Children" was born.
>
> They aren't learning disabilities. They're learning differences.
> When you change the terminology it has a positive effect on everything else.
>
> The next thing we changed was where our children learn. We didn't want to take them of a mainstream Yeshiva. So we created a program that works within a Yeshiva.
>
> After all, children learn better when they're included. Not

isolated.

Every child learns in a different way. (48)

Today, at this point in our evolving understanding of learning differences and various impairments that we as human beings have, the advocacy for this grouping in our community is so strong. If anything social pressure is such that one would not have much motivation to go against this tide. That being said, we must consider that it was not always this way.

Years ago, when I was consulting with many Jewish Day Schools, I went to a play at one of the schools in which I was present a good amount of time. This particular school was handicap-accessible as is required by the county in which it is located, a valuable model in and of itself to consider and follow. The school's drama department put on "***Fiddler on the Roof***." The school was relatively small, with less than 90 students in grades Kindergarten through Six. Every student in the school was part of the production, including a lovely young boy with Cerebral Palsy. His speech was slurred; his physical movements uncertain and he needed help walking. His part in the play was that of the Rabbi.

What the brilliant and sensitive drama director did was so powerful that I still hold it up as one of the most evolved examples of sensitive and meaningful education for the entire community two decades later. The drama teacher taught her students that the Rabbi, of course, was so honored in the community, that he had two assistants that always walked with him, holding on to his elbows. They were always ready to help him, if his Tallit fell (which actually did happen), his Kipah left his head or whatever was needed. Every time the Rabbi spoke, one of the townspeople would ask a question, repeating his words, such as "Rabbi, did you just say that we should all pray to God?" or repeat whatever it was he had said. He would shake his head affirmatively. I assure you that there was not a dry eye in the audience. All present, mostly parents and family of cast members, were most fiercely proud of their own children, to be sure, but all were beyond touched by the participation of this young student, and what this meant for him, his family and all of the members of the school family who learned so much by having him in their lives. As a Jewish educator and consultant for many years, I could only hope and wish that more of our schools and learning communities were as evolved as this one.

Let's turn our attention to the deliberations about women and their participation in the offering of the ***Hagiga***. We find ourselves on 16b of this Tractate as we enter a discussion about how one is to lay their hands on the animal they have brought for their sacrifice with all of their strength and might:

> Said Rami bar Hama: Infer ... that the laying on of the hands must be with all one's strength, because if we would imagine that all the strength is not necessary, what labor is it or what is he doing to the animal that the rabbis prohibited it on the festival? ...
>
> An objection was raised: We have learned elsewhere It is written [Lev. i. 2-4]: "Speak unto the children of Israel . . . and he shall lay his hand." *He*--the males, but not the females of Israel. R. Jose and R. Simeon, however, said that the females of Israel, if they wish, they may lay on their hands [although it is not obligatory for them]; and R. Jose added to this: My father Elazar told me that it happened once that we had a calf of peace-offering, and we brought it to the courtyard of the women, and the latter laid their hands on it. It was not because the laying on of the hands is an obligation for women, but so as to gratify them. Now, if you think that the laying on of the hand must be with all one's strength, would it be right, in order to gratify the women, to allow them to be involved with the holy things? ...

According to many who study these texts extensively, this is the pivotal text that is used to discuss and develop increased roles for women in ritual spaces in our contemporary reality, especially in the more Halachically observant sectors of the Jewish community. Notice how women are brought into those religious spaces and practices which are obligatory for men and from which they are exempt, but not forbidden. If it brings them pleasure and meaning, that is, it "gratifies them," then we are to allow them to participate. What a forward thinking point of view from so long ago!

While this may seem a less than desired or satisfactory position for those who want to use exactly the same terms for men and women; that would reflect a perspective that is within the context of another framework, not that of Halacha. For them, this may not satisfy; that being said, for those who want to work within the frame of Halachic reasoning, one has to be duly impressed by this consideration in this text, and the reasoning employed to bring women into religious spaces. Perhaps, it is worth at least a parenthetical note to state that in various religious and political traditions in our world presently, this consideration resulting in the participation and presence in public of women has still not occurred.

All of this goes to emphasize the profound importance of community. Judaism clearly values the community so much that there will often be a sense of erring on the side of caution to include everyone, or as many as absolutely possible as much as possible. To serve as a powerful example, of particular note is a teaching from another tractate of the Talmud, that of **Pesachim**. We are looking at the discourse focused on the participation in the sacrifices, practices and celebrations involved with the annual celebration of **Pesach** or Passover (49). Our example comes from the statement of a rather remarkable position within the midst of a lengthy discussion in the complicated instructions regarding offering of the Pesach sacrifice, which is incumbent upon all members of the B'nai Yisrael, both as individuals and as members of the group.

There are two specific teachings in these sets of laws that are particularly noteworthy in their relevance to this primary focus on community. First, the Pesach offering is to be offered in **Chaburot**, or in groups, in which individual members are to be registered for a specific Pesach sacrifice. Secondly, the Pesach is to be offered in a state of **Tehorah** and those who are individually **Tamei** can delay their involvement until **Pesach Sheni**. However, if the community as a whole or a reasonable number of members of the community are **Tamei**, then one insures that this is the case with the majority of the group, even going so far as to intentionally have an additional group member touch something that is ***Tamei***; and then the offering is given with the majority in this state of ritual impurity. Why? Because the importance of group participation trumps individual states of ritual purity! This is not to say that the latter is not important, just not so core as to invalidate participation of the masses.

A word about language and how it has a profound on our understanding of community is in order here. Rabbi Avi Weiss teaches that ***Tamei/Tum'ah*** is an example of a term that cannot be adequately translated in terms of the contextual understanding of what it conveys. To call this "ritual impurity" can and indeed becomes potentially explosive when translated and interpreted into other languages and contexts. Specifically, if one is excluded because of some level of ritual impurity than this becomes a blight on the person. This is not the intention, not in rooted meaning and not in the spirit of the use of the term. Rabbi Weiss cites Rav Aharon Soleveichik, who uses the sense of permanence or temporality to distinguish between what is ***Tahor*** and what is ***Tamei***. In this discussion at hand about the importance of the group, which is seen as permanent and everlasting, as well as their connection to God, also thus seen; it therefore makes sense that while we want to remove that which is not permanent but temporary, such as a blemish or skin rash; it is more important and therefore the clear priority to protect the integrity of the group and its collective experience, which we hope and anticipate will last.

Given this caveat and its implications about the importance of the group, let us think about this carefully. Is everyone truly welcome in our community of faith and belief and practice? Are we "erring on the side of caution" in insuring that everyone is able to participate with us in our community to the degree they desire and are able? Do we apply necessary limits of inclusion with kindness and compassion and within the narrowest necessary limitations?

Recently a dear friend (and the mother of my son-in-law) sent me a wonderful and meaningful email, which features Nicholas Ferroni, an educator and activist. There is a picture of this nice looking man with the following statement that appears next to his picture, which one may or may not use to make assumptions about his life and sexuality, as one begins reading the text, which is positioned vertically as follows next to his picture.

> "I was born a sinner too.
>
> My sin is mentioned in the Bible 25 times.
>
> I tried to change, but couldn't...
>
> Luckily society learned to accept
>
> us left-handed people."

I laughed and felt such empathy with the author of this statement, as I too am left-handed. I have been so my entire life and I don't anticipate this changing any time soon. Years ago, my daughter Rachie shared a wonderful Shiyur that she attended given by Rav Ethan Tucker when she was a student at Yeshivat Hadar in New York. When she explained the general contours of the Shiyur with me, I knew that here was a special message from important texts that are relevant to her, myself, Nicholas Ferroni and all other left-handed people in our world. We were indeed considered sinister, outside of the norm and rather shady creatures in many places and spaces throughout history.

First of all, for all of us who are left-handed (and over the age of 50 something), we remember teachers trying to "get us" to be right-handed. It was thought that something was WRONG with you if you were left-handed. There are many, many (too many really) studies in which this was attempted (and failed miserably, in case you were wondering).

So to return to our Jewish texts, in the Gemara, left-handedness is AN ISSUE, actually a BIG issue in terms of when and how one could be included in the community. Rabbi Tucker, and by association, Rachie identified four models of what should be done with these left-handed oddities. Here I will extrapolate what I have

232

learned as I myself have gone through these and other texts from the Jewish tradition.

In the first model, we look at the Kohanim who had to perform certain prescribed functions in the sacrificial rites for the B'nai Yisrael. There are specific elements of this very clearly articulated and disciplined ritual practice that required right-handed Kohanim. The question is what if the Kohan (who already is in an exclusive and specific group that excludes so many others in the community) was in fact left-handed? The answer is that the Kohan is OUT for these sacrificial rights and cannot perform this function. It does not however invalidate his inherited identity as a Kohan, nor that of his children and future generations. (Masechet Bechorot 45b, Talmud Bavli).

In the second model, we consider the beautiful pageantry of the processions in which all members of the community carried their Lulavim and Etrogim. What if someone is left-handed? Does he (and remember for the purposes of these texts and their discussions, we are only speaking of the men in the community) then reverse how he carries the Arba'ah Minim (the Lulav and Etrog)? Oh no, we are taught, for the purposes of community unity, everyone should carry the Lulav and Etrog as one would do if they were right-handed. Do not reverse how these are carried, for that would ruin the beautiful aesthetics of the sight of the entire community marching in unison. That is, all should look the same, devoid of individual differences to produce some pre-determined sense of beauty. (Sukkah 37b, Talmud Bavli)

The third model is based on the wearing of Tefilin. In the Gemara (Masechet Menachot 37a – 37b, Talmud Bavli), there is a discussion about what a left-handed person should do regarding the wearing of the Tefilin on their arm. According to Halacha, the arm that was generally used was the left arm, so that right-handed people could wrap their Tefilin and they could be worn on the weak arm, the left hand, which would not be used to do so much anyway. The problem is (especially since in days of old, people might wear their Tefilin all day) how can one have one's strong arm (if they are left-handed) encumbered in such a manner – they would not be able to get any meaningful work done! So the suggestion is offered that one should read the original instructions as indicating that one should wear the Tefilin on their weaker arm, and in this case, one's normal strong left arm is analogous to the conventional normal strong right arm; and the right weaker arm for the left-handed person is analogous to the left weaker arm for the right-handed person. In this model, each individual gets to take the following approach: Here my **normal** way of doing whatever I am doing may and is different from your way, but just as good and appropriate within the context of my identity.

The fourth model is based on the legal discussion about the prohibition of writing. In Shabbat 103a, Rabbi Jeremiah conducts a discussion about whether or not the prohibition of writing two letters together refers to only writing with the right hand (considered the normative hand for doing so) or also with the left hand (that is to say, the hand one would not normally use, assuming he like all others is right-handed!). Here the conclusion is that whatever hand one uses generally is the one that he/she is prohibited to write with, and if one is ambidextrous, than one cannot use either hand.

In this articulation of these four models, notice that we do not unequivocally exclude the left-handed person. Rather there are different degrees of accommodation, ranging from considering the left-handed person's normal mode of being as analogous to the normative identity that is assumed for the general population to exclusion from specific actions that must be done in a prescribed and specific manner. Similarly, in Masechet Hagiga, we are interfacing the elements of the offering itself, importance of community and suitability of those that participate in the community on the occasion of the offering, which **all** are obligated to do. In looking at all components, the Rabbis of the Mishnah and the Talmud try to include everyone possible as much as possible, to enhance the community, as well as to bring fulfillment to individuals. This is a wonderful model of community building. How can we apply this model in our world today, certainly in Jewish religious spaces, in other religious spaces, political spaces, and other types of communities, which may not be as "welcoming" as they would like to think that they are or need to be?

We discussed the notion of intentional actions and involvement elsewhere in these essays and here we see that the intentional focus is on the people involved in the experience and in fulfilling Mitzvot, which is always seen as a preferable way to be in Jewish Law. To go even further, we have the rather remarkable example from Masechet Pesachim where it is suggested that we go so far as to insure that a majority of a given community is "spiritually impure" so that together they can indeed participate in a dictated offering. Clearly, this is an opposite approach to those who would exclude too many people from our community too quickly due to lessened skills of intellect, various infirmities, age, sexuality or gender identity and too many other criteria.

Rabbi Elliot Dorff proposes such an approach in a rather provocative essay on how we regard disabilities and differences. (50) He begins by citing the blessing we say thanking God for creating different beings (***Mishaneh HaBriyot***) and proposes what he calls a "Copernican Revolution" by thinking of ourselves as ***temporarily abled*** but ultimately and potentially among the disabled. If we were to somehow be able to see and absorb the reality of our existence from the point of view of so many cited in the beginning of the Talmudic text cited in this chapter from ***Hagiga***, then we would redefine who community is and those in the community. His point in challenging us to engage in this thought exercise is to realize that in this setting the "other" would become us. Can we do this? Dare we do this on any level regarding this or any other set of concerns that reflect our "otherness" and non-binary state of being?

Let us all imagine for a moment what would happen if we were to use the models indicated here, which are focused on the greatest degree to which one can participate in community as much as possible. Can we read our texts and consider various understandings of our sources, intended to guide us in purposeful living more than exclusion of each other from various spaces!

As Henry David Thoreau is so well known for saying, "Things don't change, we do." It is incumbent upon us to ask honestly what our texts, our faiths, our codes of behavior and discipline and other instructive sources to which we are beholden are asking us to do and to remember that we may have to, as our Rabbis did so long ago, wrestle with ourselves until we realize that our community and collective is not just what we want it to be, but determined by outside sources and instructions that may not serve our individually vested purposes. What we do at that point is up to us, as it was for Avraham and so many others that provide us with models of meaningful community, kind inclusion of many, and intentional living individually and collectively.

Questions for Continued Thought and Discussion:

1. Did you learn any new approaches of inclusion in community from the Jewish sources cited here?

2. What are these new approaches and how can and will you apply them in your life? Where?

3. Does the perspective here bring a new dimension to your understanding of what it means to be religiously observant in terms of how we build community?

4. What is the most important lesson that you take from reading this book and how will you use it in your life?

Afterword

Our discussion does not end here. It is hoped that all of us will continue to think intentionally as we look at the myriad of challenges in our lives as human beings and how we can apply lessons from our religious traditions to our lives today in a meaningful and compassionate way. It is my belief that religion asks us to be the best we can be and to try to engender that in others. This is **not** the tone of too much of the extremist expressions of religious doctrine we see in our world today.

As Margaret Mead teaches, it is up to each of us to do our part in this world. It is hoped that these writings have inspired all of us to think about what that part is for each of us and to join hands, both literally and figuratively, in working to make our world a better and less fractured place for us, our children and for many generations to come. In so doing, it is my hope that religion will once again become the *Of Course!* in many people's lives, bringing the support and elevation that can only serve to make us better human beings.

I hope that this discussion will continue in your own minds, as you consider how we help to repair our fractured world with those you love and in our communities of discourse with the many different voices that comprise the totality of that community.

Appendix I: Endnotes and Sources to Consult for More Information

An Introductory Word or Two

(1) Cultural anthropologists have long studied the elements that define a society and religion is clearly a central factor. For a brief survey of this work, the reader is referred to Encyclopedia of Religion and Society, William H. Swatos, Editor. USA: Hartford Institute, for Religion Research, hirr@hartsem.edu.

(2) Ken Nerburn in his important collection of teachings in The Wisdom of the Native Americans (California: New World Library, 1999) relates in writing stories and lore of the Native Americans. There was a great controversy regarding committing to writing these generationally transmitted stories through telling, such an important element of the continuation of the Native American culture and community. Pages 3 – 4 are quoted here.

(3) Pew Research, Religion and Public Life Project, January 8, 2014.

Chapter One: Stepping Back and Moving Forward

(4) Please note that all references in Tanach/Jewish Bible reflect no one translation in particular, but a mixture of those that best reflect the true meaning of the original Hebrew text. Further, note that God is always referenced as such without any pronouns, which reflect a limitation of language often resulting in deep theological discussions about the gender of God which this author considers to be a non-issue, that is to say that God does not have a gender nor any other limiting physical characteristic. Finally, license has been taken by this author to provide translations that reflect the contextual meaning of the words, rather than exact literal word for word translations.

(5) Tom Cahill, <u>The Gifts of the Jews,</u> New York: Doubleday, 1998. This is an important book written by a non-Jew that looks at Judaism within the context of world history and lasting lessons this people/culture/religion has bestowed upon our collective and shared generations of experience and journeying. This book is one of a series written by Cahill about various cultural/national/religious groupings and is highly recommended to the reader if this study interests you. Quoted phrases come from pages 53 and 63 respectively.

(6) Cahill, p. 63

(7) Melanie A. Greenberg, Ph.D., *"Turning to the Positive: Personal Growth After Trauma,"* <u>Psychology Today</u>, March 4, 2013; found at http://www.psychologytoday.com/blog/the-mindful-self-express/201303/turning-the-positive-personal-growth-after-trauma/comments

(8) Khalid Duran (with Abdelwahib Hechiche), <u>Children of Abraham: An Introduction to Islam for Jews</u> (U.S.A.: Ktav Publishing House: 2001), pp. 17 – 18.

(9) As stories from the Midrash and similar sources are recounted, the actual source will be indicated in the text itself. Again, license has been taken by this author to

provide translations that reflect the contextual meaning of the words, rather than exact literal word for word translations.

Chapter Two: Roots and Wings

(10) Nerburn, The Wisdom of the Native Americans, pp. 14 – 17.

(11) While this notion of generational transmission, to be discussed fully in these essays appears often in the Torah, Talmud and in so many classical Jewish texts, as an example, Shabbat 22b is referenced here.

(12) Robert Bly, The Sibling Society, (U.S.A.: Addison-Wesley Publishing co., 1996), p. 132.

(13) Victor Barnouw, An Introduction to Anthropology (United States of America: The Dorsey Press, 1971), p. 117. A huge problem and challenge is that the family unit has been in one way or another the primary social unit for most cultures as studied by cultural anthropologists. The family may take different formats but in every case, whether nuclear, tribal or otherwise, transmission of teachings and values from older generations to those who are younger is a well-known and commonly found feature. It is this pattern that Bly fears is threatened.

(14) Charles Kimball discusses this phenomenon of the abuses and misuses of religion in our world at length in his book, When Religion Becomes Evil (New York: Harper Collins, 2002); this quote is from p.1.

(15) Irshad Manji, The Trouble with Islam (New York: St. Martin's Press, 2003, p. 30.

(16) The Twelve Step Program was incepted in Christian circles, serving to address the complete alienation of the individual, loss of self, lack of group membership and finally, lack of belief in a Higher Power. For a brief listing of these twelve steps, go to http://12step.org/the-12-steps . Note that this version of the 12 steps is an adaptation from the original 12 Steps of Alcoholics Anonymous by the administrator of the indicated web site and can be adapted in addressing any addictive or dysfunctional behavior.

Chapter Three: Free Choice or Informed Choice?

(17) Anuradha Ketaria , Democracy on Trial: All Rise (United States of America: Algora Publishing, 2011), quoted text here is on p. 87. This is part of a larger discussion on the irony of use of choice to limit choice. Why and how does this happen? The author goes on to show how rule of the majority is often **not** rule for the benefit of the majority and how this often happens as a reaction to many factors which leaders use to instill fear of individual choice of destiny which would compromise the well-being of the people generally.

(18) Gerald L. Schroeder, Ph.D., Genesis and the Big Bang (New York: Bantam Books, 1990), pp. 150 – 151. It should be stated that many scientists, who are also members of faith community leadership and clergy, address this topic. Not all scientists and not all people of

faith are comfortable with this work and leverage charges of compromising both fields of endeavor. However, for those who are willing to entertain how to interface the discussion from these two very different venues, these works are quite helpful and informative.

(19) Rabbi Harold Kushner, When Bad Things Happen to Good People, (U.S.A.: Schocken Books, 1981). In his book Kushner sets out three statements as being the litmus test for what is true about God and us when considering the difficult complexities of theodicy. He states them as follows: (a) God is all powerful and caused everything that happens in the world; (b) God is just and fair and insures that the good prosper and the wicked suffer; and (c) People – actually the Biblical persona of Job in Kushner's schema – are good. He comes to the point where all three cannot be true and processes different approaches to theodicy in the form of Job's friends through the prism of these three statements.

(20) Information about J.C. Philpot and his sermons can be found at http://www.gracegems.org/sermons.htm

Chapter Four: Rules and Regulations

(21) Rabbi Jonathan Sacks, To Heal a Fractured World: The Ethics of Responsibility, (New York: Schocken Books, 2005), p. 239. Rabbi Sacks discusses at length the notion that there is so much in Jewish Law that engenders and mandates responsibility and concern for others; but the individual must internalize these qualities in order to properly understand the reasons and foundational basis

242

for all of the rules and regulations that are part of the system of Jewish Law. Within the context of the story he shares, even in tying one's shoes there are instructions that are related to who and what we are as human beings; if we give intentional thought to such small actions, how much more so will we do just that regarding the much larger issues in our lives?

(22) This statement is found in a reading that explains critical issues about the Native Americans and their lives; as well as how they are threatened in the present reality of the United States. This can be found at http://indigenousfoundations.arts.ubc.ca/home/culture/oral-traditions.html

(23) Yeshayahu Leibowitz, Judaism, Human Values, and the Jewish State, Eliezer Goldman, edit., Cambridge: Harvard University Press, 1995, p. 12. As a side note, Leibowitz was a biochemist by training and profession, as are many other important writers and thinkers of contemporary Jewish philosophy, he integrates the various areas of his experience and expertise in crafting the placement of where Jewish Law as an entity and its dictates fits realistically into our lives.

Chapter Five: When My Childhood Is Your History

(24) Robert Bly, The Sibling Society, p. 230. Bly's point is that with fractured generational transmission, the continuity of society and the ongoing practice of its rules and regulations as well as cultural markers are severely compromised.

(25) Irving Howe, <u>World of our Fathers</u>, (New York: Harcourt Brace Jovanovich, 1976), p. 180.

(26) Dan Jones, <u>The Summer of Blood: The Peasants' Revolt of 1381,</u> (England: UK General Books, 2010). Here is an extensive discussion of what can go terribly wrong when wronged generations will rebel against previously held power. Jones try to provide historical perspective and reconsider what the goals of the rebellion were and what were the noble causes that were intended to protect the coming generations of British history.

(27) Robert Bly, <u>The Sibling Society</u>, Chapter Two of his book is entitled ***Jack, the Beanstalk, and the Giant with a Large Appetite***, pp. 8 – 43. Bly shows how the giant once stood for all those things that were not honorable and not to be set up as goals; hopefully to be obliterated by the powers of good. However, children left to themselves develop the type of entitlement that is too often devoid of accountability and the sense of connectedness and gratitude to those before them, and instead see themselves as the potential giant with a large appetite.

Chapter Six: Me and We

(28) The fuller discussion by Rabbi Sacks appears in a variety of venues as reprinted from his collection of weekly Torah studies on his web site, www.rabbisacks.org

(29) Koran, Sura VII: 57 – 62 (Al Araf) – It is so interesting to note that for Muslims, Noach becomes very important

with regard to these cited attempts to get the people of his generation to change. Noach is justified in these attempts as is the destruction of the masses who did not heed his call.

(30) The Torah: A Modern Commentary with commentaries by W. Gunther Plaut, United States: Union of American Hebrew Congregations, 1981, pp. 126 – 127.

(31) *Chapter 8: Societal Changes Force Rapid Human Services Changes (1960s)*, Alliance for Strong Families and Communities, at http://alliance1.org/centennial/book/revolutionary-societal-changes-force-rapid-human-services-changes-1960s is one example of a discussion that shows how societal forces brought powerful change and new initiative as a result of rebellion and dissatisfaction.

Chapter Seven: Values and Actions

(32) For a full examination of this important movement and its teachers and teachings, see Rabbi Israel Salanter and the Musar Movement: Seeking the Torah of Truth by Immanuel Etkes (United States: The Jewish Publication Society, 1993).

Chapter Eight: Passion or Compassion

(33) While many teachings could have been chosen, these were decided upon, as they can stand alone out of their

context for our purposes. However, please note that there are clearly premises for these teachings that are problematic for Jews, as there is a premise that much of the misdeeds and wrongdoings which Jesus protests are attributed to the Pharisees, the most prevalent Jewish movement, if you will, of the time. While these charges may not necessarily and easily appear as easily dismissible, our purpose here is not to engage in an historical discussion of what did or did not happen and what is or is not a salient historical argument; but rather to point to the fact that compassionate living is the desired goal here, as it is in the Tanach and will be seen in the Qu'ran as well. The texts from Matthew and Colossians are adapted and quoted from The Holy Bible: Revised Standard Version, Herbert G. May and Bruce M. Metzger, editors (New York: Oxford University Press, 1973).

(34) As indicated in #33 above, many different texts could have been chosen, but taking a verse or two out of context is always tricky and something I generally resist doing. However, what is being presented here is that the three Monotheistic religious texts share this ideal of compassionate living, albeit not always achieving the stated goals. Note here must be made that submission to Allah is part of the equation as is faith in Jesus for the Christian community. All texts from the Qu'ran and New Testament's Gospels must be read accordingly within that context. Notice that as I often state, every translation is necessarily an interpretation; this is noted in the very title of this source. The Koran Interpreted, A Translation by A.J. Arberry, (United States: Simon and Schuster, 1996).

(35) Allan Gould, <u>What Did They Think of the Jews</u>, (United States: Jason Aronson, Inc, 1990), pp. 71 – 72. This has been oft-quoted and can be found in any number of sources; this particular one has value as it is a rather broad historical perspective on Jewish influence and input in our history.

(36) Rabbi Jonathan Sacks, <u>The Great Partnership: Science, Religion and the Search for Meaning</u>, (New York: Schocken Books, 2011), p. 252.

Chapter Nine: A Few Important and Timeless Teachers

(37) Jason Sherman, ***Patience***, (Canada: Playwrights Canada Press, 2000).

(38) Archibald MacLeish, <u>JB: A Play in Verse</u>, (United States: Houghton Mifflin, 1989); the play won the Pulitzer Prize for best drama in 1959.

Chapter Ten: Soft Souls in a Rough World

(39) This dynamic is discussed in great length by Peter F. Carbone in his treatment of Harold Rugg, a most important educational thinker who truly pushed and believed in the potential of the institution of school to function as a force for change in our society, by educating its students to live by important ideals. Peter F. Carbone, Jr., <u>The Social and Educational Thought of Harold Rugg</u>, (Durham, N.C.: Duke University Press, 1977).

(40) Words of "For Good" from *Wicked*, Stephen Schwartz, 2003. This was written as a result of inspiration from a conversation Schwartz had with his daughter about her best friend, asking what she would want to say to her if she knew she was never going to see her again.

Chapter Eleven: The Greatest Teacher of All – The Power Above Us All

(41) Sagan often addresses this interfacing of believing in what we may not be able to prove what is as opposed to what we see and can supposedly prove to be so, even though, as we know all too well, this too will change. Stephen Hawking, <u>A Brief History of Time</u> (New York: Bantam Books, 1988), p. x.

(42) Clearly, so many statements of this ilk could be included here. Einstein's is well known and Luzzato carefully develops this premise in his book, <u>The Way of God</u> at great length and in painfully small steps in his world of the eighteenth century. (U.S.A. : Philip Feldheim Publishers, 2009)

(43) Stephen Spielberg, <u>Close Encounters of the Third Kind</u> (New York: Dell, 1977), pp. 190 – 191.

Chapter Twelve: Achdut – Accepting and Appreciating the Gifts We All Bring

(44) This translation is from Yusaf Ali and occurs within the context of a discussion about forbidden foods, somewhat echoing words of VaYikra/Leviticus in terms of what is not to be eaten. Also indicated here is the notion of

others giving up illusions of alternative beliefs. It is interesting to think about this concept and compare it to the discussion above about the verse from Zechariah about the future vision of the desired outcome of our existence here according to Jewish belief.

Chapter Thirteen: A Model from the Past and Reality of the Present

(45) Bertrand Russell, The Problems of Philosophy, (U.S.A.: Wilder Publications, 2007 edition, originally published in 1912), pp. 93 – 94.

(46) Rabbi Hayim HaLevy Donin, To Be A Jew, New York, Basic Books, 1972, p. 35. It should be pointed out that this is a very practical "how to" book as its title suggests. While providing a foundation of thought and approach to this life of doing, it is the practical stuff of the things we do that is the topic and the goal of this work.

(47) Please note that all translations are indeed interpretations as is the case at all times when texts are not presented in their language of origin. These translations are my own, compiled from several sources including Schottenstein Babylonian Talmud translations, those from the modern Hebrew explanations of Adin Steinsaltz and others. These translations are mine alone and some additional information that is presumed in the original text is sometimes included for context. Please note that this disclaimer should be applied to this entire chapter.

(48) To consider how people once viewed our children with learning differences and disabilities and the lack of initiative in providing for them in too many of our Jewish communities is relevant in that so much of these prejudices have changed and evolved. PTACH has been pivotal in doing so and it should be noted that such change of perspective takes time and the effort of many. This is a model of just such effort and involvement that is worth considering as we continue to attempt to be as inclusive as possible and do so, for those who wish to, within the parameters of Halachic reasoning.

(49) In Masechet Pesachim of the Babylonian Talmud, this lengthy discussion begins on 80b and continues throughout Chapter Seven; there are many side conversations as well in which several options to insure maximal participation in the offering of the Paschal offering on either Pesach or Pesach Sheni is hopefully facilitated. This compelling option truly indicates the primary importance of community and participation of all individuals in the community, trumping to a degree the notion of spiritual purity.

(50) Rabbi Elliot Dorff, <u>Mishaneh Ha-Briyyot: A New Jewish Approach to Disabilities</u>, New York: The United Synagogue of Conservative Judaism, http://www.uscj.org/JewishLivingandLearning/SocialAction/Accessibility/MishanehHaBriyyotANewJewishApproachtoDisabilities.aspx

Appendix II: Glossary of Hebrew Terms

Achdut – unity of the Jewish nation, acknowledging that there are many differences and variations amongst the individuals and groupings that make up this larger community.

Achrayut – responsibility that is often talked about within Jewish law that Jews have for each other, extending to the responsibility that human beings have in being invested in other members of the human family of which we are all part.

Adam – the human being that is created by God, containing both elements of the ground (see next word) and elements specifically from God.

Adamah – the ground, from which the human being is created by God.

Ahavat Yisrael – love for all members of the Jewish nation, this is the opposite of causeless hatred **(Sinat Hinam)** that breaks down and destroys human interactions and community well-being.

Ahavat Olam – love for all nations and individuals of the worldwide community, for ultimately all people are created by and in the image of the One and Only One God.

Akedat Yitzchak – the binding of Isaac, the defining moment in the life of Abraham/Avraham and in Jewish/monotheistic history at which we learn that God does not want, nor does God allow child sacrifice for any reason.

Aleinu – *Tefillah*/prayer at the end of daily services that reminds us of our need to praise the One and Only One God, called the martyr's prayer as many Jews say this as the last proclamation before death.

Aseret HaDibrot – Ten Commandments, or the most basic set of laws indicated in the Torah to which all monotheistic religions that are rooted in this story adhere.

Ba'al Teshuvah – a Jew that was religious, moved away from thee roots and practices and then returned; in modern parlance this term is used generally for anyone who takes on additional practices or **Mitzvot**, nonetheless historically speaking most, if not virtually all, of us are **Ba'alei Teshuvah**.

Bechirah Chofshit – free and informed choice, the special and dedicated element and capacity of the human species that distinguishes and defines us.

Beracha – A blessing with a set formula that is said before partaking of food or drink or before engaging in any number of activities; also the central element of Jewish prayer.

BeTzelem Elokim – in the image of God, what we are told about how the human being was created in the beginning chapters of the Torah.

Halacha – the content and process of Jewish law and the development of the detailed observance of stated commandments, or *Mitzvot.*

Hashevat Aveidah – the commandment to return what is lost to the owner and to make an honest and concerted attempt to do so.

Hesed – deeds of kindness we are commanded to show towards each other as we are all made in the image of God, **BeTzelem Elokim.**

Heshbon HaNefesh – the taking account of self that is an intrinsic part of Jewish Law and Living.

Hillul HaShem – desecration of the name of God through improper actions and behaviors, especially problematic when cloaked with self-righteous satisfaction in being religiously observant.

Kashrut – the system of dietary laws prescribed in Torah and Rabbinic literature, maintained by many religious and ritualistically observant Jews.

Kehilah – Jewish community, our collection of Jewish souls that make up our people, this term can also be used to refer to a specific Jewish community or grouping.

Kibbud Av v'Em – honor for one's father and mother, a central *Mitzvah,* the fifth of the *Aseret HaDibrot.*

Kibbud HaBeriot – honor and respect for all human beings created by God; this is an imperative standard that is often emphasized.

Kibbud HaShem – honor and respect for God; accompanied by other standards of respect and honor; clearly it is most important to show this respect for God, but we should remember that it is through actual actions and concern showed for all that God has created that we give honor to The Creator.

Kiddush – the prayer said over wine at the beginning of meals of gathering in Jewish observance and living, for example, on Shabbat and all Festivals. This prayer sanctifies or sets apart the meal as special. On other occasions, a simple *Beracha* or blessing over the drinking of wine is appropriate.

Lifnei Meshurat HaDin – going above and beyond the requirements of Jewish law in maintaining the highest possible standards of (in this case) behavior and ethics.

Malchut Yisrael – the Kingdom of Israel, the period of the Kings and the Prophets narrated in the Tanach/Jewish Bible.

Midat Rachamim – the strict attribute of compassion and caring according to which God judges action and we are enjoined to do the same.

MiDor LeDor – Jewish law, behaviors and standards are passed down from one generation to the next generation and in turn to those that follow.

Midot – Strict measurable ethical standards that are part of the system of *Mitzvah*

Minyan – generally a prayer grouping that joins together in the Jewish community, specifically the minimum acceptable number for this prayer community is ten (men only in the Orthodox community, men and women in the other ideological movements).

Mitzvah/Mitzvot – commanded action/s that are indicated in the Torah and explained more fully and further developed in the Mishna and Gemara, parts of the Talmud.

Mitzvot Bein Adam LeChavero – the category of commanded actions that structure how we relate to each other, amongst ourselves as human beings and as members of the Jewish people.

Mitzvot Bein Adam LaMakom – the category of commanded actions that structure how we relate to God.

Musar – a movement in the later nineteenth century that was focused on proper behavior and motivation for doing the various *Mitzvot* and living a Jewish life, specifically on ethical reasoning for how we live and the details of that life.

Nefesh – The soul of a human being that makes them human.

Neshamah – The inner soul that is placed in the human being, when God breathes into the human being's nostrils in Chapter Two of Genesis. **Neshimah** is the Hebrew word for breath.

Or LaGoyim – the prophetic vision of Israel's place in the world as a light to the other nations by virtue of proper behaviors and showing that Israel is worthy of such a position

Pesach -- the spring festival that celebrates the most defining experience of the Jewish nation in becoming such, namely, the Exodus from Egypt and the life of slavery there, as well as readiness to become a people invested in the serving of God through our own choice.

Rambam – Moshe ben Maimon or Maimonides lived from 1138 until 1204 and was a renowned scholar and teacher as well as a respected physician. He is known for his codification of Jewish law in his *Mishna Torah* and his application as well as further explanation of many of its laws. *Hilchot Tefillah* or the Laws of Prayer is part of the all-encompassing *Mishna Torah.*

Sefirat HaOmer – the period of time between *Pesach* and *Shavuot* of 49 days that join the festival that celebrates our freedom from slavery and the festival that celebrates our accepting the responsibility and observance of Torah in our lives; a period of some restricted activity for many Jews.

Shabbat – The Sabbath for the Jewish community observed from sundown on Friday until after sunset on Saturday, for a length of time a bit more than 25 hours or so.

Shavuot – The festival that comes at the beginning of summer that celebrates the Giving of our Torah and our acceptance of the responsibility and joy of its observance.

Shema – the most well-known and central prayer of Jewish faith, proclaiming the Absolute Oneness of God for all times, also speaks of various aspects of the relationship between Jews and God and what each does in this relationship.

Shemoneh Esrei – also called the *Amidah*, this prayer is at the core of each of the three daily services with a combination of *Berachot*/blessings of praise, requests, and thanks to God for all that we have in our lives.

Shiluach Kan – the commanded action of sending a mother bird away from her net before taking eggs from it.

Shlichut – the mission we are given in our lives here in this world to help and use our talents to build a better world.

Shmirat HaLashon – a system of laws that govern how we speak and use words in our interactions with each other.

Sinat Hinam – Causeless hatred of another, we are told this is the reason for the destruction of the Second Temple and we are to strive for love of our fellow human beings and members of the Jewish nation, *Ahavat Olam* and *Ahavat Yisrael*.

Sukkot – the fall harvest festival during which many Jews build and dwell in *Sukkot* as we observe and acknowledge dependence on God and all that has been created for our benefit.

Tahor – The state of ritual purity is desired in various Jewish practices.

Tahara – The washing of a body after death to elevate the individual's soul to a state of purity.

Talmud – classical Rabbinic codes that are seen by those who are more observant as having the same authority as Torah; the degree of authority ascribed to the **Talmud** is one of the most compelling differences among different denominational groupings in the Jewish community.

Tamei – The state of ritual impurity, which can be remedied according to dictates of Jewish law.

Tefillah – prayer is a primary aspect of the lives of many Jews and is our communication channel with God.

Torah – the source of laws and practices and history that is considered the primary text for Jews, various groupings in the Jewish community attribute varying degrees of authority to it and question source of its authorship; nonetheless its central position is addressed one way or another by all Jews.

Tum'ah – A source or thing that renders an individual *Tamei* or spiritually impure.

Umot HaOlam – nations of the world, it is foundational in Jewish teaching to have respect and regard for others outside of the Jewish nation as well.

Yetzer HaRa – One of the two inclinations that are given to the human being, generally described as the evil inclination, but can also be seen as the creative urge.

Yetzer Tov – One of the two inclinations that are given to the human being, generally described as the good inclination, spurring us on to do right.

Yichud HaShem – the most foundational belief of Judaism is the Absolute Oneness of our One and Only One God.

Yom Tov – a holiday or festival, such as several that have been mentioned in this text.

Zachor – the commanded action to remember what has happened to us as Jews and how we are to observe, something we do through the annual cycle of our observances, daily prayers, weekly cycle of life, our texts, and so much of daily Jewish living.

Zeman Cheiruteinu – the time of our freedom from slavery in Egypt, this is one of the alternate names of ***Pesach.***

Zeman Matan Torateinu – the time of receiving the gift of our *Torah*, this is one of the alternate names of ***Shavuot.***

Zeman Simchateinu – the time of our joyfulness, this is one of the alternate names of ***Sukkot.***

Zichrono/ah LeShalom – "may his/her name be for a blessing or for peace" is what we often say after mention of the name of someone who has died.

Made in the USA
Middletown, DE
27 April 2021